DESPERATE WIVES

DESPERATE WIVES

Brenda Clayton

Help and Hope for Women Considering Separation or Divorce

BEACON HILL PRESS
OF KANSAS CITY

Copyright 2006
by Brenda Clayton and Beacon Hill Press of Kansas City

ISBN-13: 978-0-8341-2238-3
ISBN-10: 0-8341-2238-3

Printed in the
United States of America

Cover Design: Brandon R. Hill
Interior Design: Sharon Page

Library of Congress Cataloging-in-Publication Data

Clayton, Brenda, 1952-
Desperate wives : help and hope for women considering separation or divorce / Brenda Clayton.
p. cm.
Includes bibliographical references.
ISBN-13: 978-0-8341-2238-3 (pbk.)
ISBN-10: 0-8341-2238-3 (pbk.)
1. Marriage—Religious aspects—Christianity. 2. Divorce—Religious aspects—Christianity. 3. Christian women—Religious life. I. Title.

BT706.C53 2006
248.8'435—dc22

2006013683

10 9 8 7 6 5 4 3 2 1

For my grandmother, Hope, and my mother, Georgene

ACKNOWLEDGMENTS

Thanks to my husband, Dayne, and our children, Travis, Ryan, Darren, Jamie, and Garrett, for their love, support, and encouragement.

Thanks to my church family at Hilltop Community Church in Carson City, Nevada (especially the "Glory Gals" Women's Ministry group).

Thanks to author Liz Curtis Higgs who was the guest speaker at the first writers conference I ever attended—Mount Hermon Christian Writers Conference in Mount Hermon, California.

Thanks to my publisher, Bonnie Perry, and my editor, Judi Perry, of Beacon Hill Press of Kansas City.

CONTENTS

HOW DID I GET HERE?

I rounded the corner leading to the women's rest room to check the prayer request boxes placed there for the weekend marriage conference. The young woman was standing alone in the rest room, crying softly.

As I slowly walked toward her, I glanced at her name tag. I knew immediately who she was. Earlier in the day we received a written prayer request from her husband. He wrote that she had left him and was living with another man. He had convinced her to attend the conference in the hope that she would be persuaded to come home to him and their three children.

Her arms were folded defensively across her body. She was very pretty, with long, brown hair that fell in soft curls below her shoulders. I asked if she was all right. She said in a quiet but firm voice, "No. I don't want to be here." I asked if I could talk to her or pray with her. She shook her head. "I can't do this," she said. I thought if I kept

11

trying to reach out to her, she might soften. I asked if she had children. "Three. Two boys and a girl."

After a minute, she sobbed, "I *just* can't do this!" I knew I had only a moment to impact her in a positive way, so I gently touched her folded arms and said, "Why don't you spend the rest of the day with me and we'll talk about it?"

Even though I had never met her before, I could say those words because I *knew* her— her heart, her mind, and her thoughts. She was me nearly 20 years earlier. I also had three children—two boys and a girl. I had abandoned my marriage because of bitterness, frustration, and anger. I felt totally justified in my feelings and just as unmovable as this young wife and mother. My heart sank. She didn't come with me. We continued to pray for this couple and their marriage throughout the weekend, but I never saw her again.

Of course, not every woman considering separation or divorce is having an affair or even considering one. But for one reason or another she feels bitter, isolated, angry, and wants out. If that is where you find yourself today, this book can offer you a fresh approach to your marriage and hope for the satisfaction and fulfillment you anticipated on your wedding day.

However, if you are in a marriage where there is physical, sexual, or emotional abuse, this book is not for you. It is your responsibility to preserve your own safety and that of your children by removing yourself from the situation. Anyone who advises you to stay in an abusive situation does not have your best interest at heart.

Your Heart Condition

As Dr. Randy Carlson points out in his book *Starved for Affection,* many couples live what Henry David Thoreau described so poignantly in his book *Walden* as "lives of quiet desperation."[1]

In the past, my husband, Dayne, and I served in youth ministry. I often counseled and prayed with teenaged girls troubled by personal problems and family difficulties. Some girls were so distraught they were crying and I couldn't always understand what they were saying. One evening while straining to hear the anguished words of a young girl, God gave me a picture of her heart. I saw a real, beating, flesh-and-blood human heart—not like a Valentine heart. And wrapped around her heart was barbed wire like the concertina wire coiled across the top of prison fences. It was wound tightly and digging into her heart. It was a picture of what was happening in her life, and I felt I understood her circumstances even though I'd never met her before. That picture gave me a focus of how to pray for her.

So let me ask you, what does your heart look like right now? Let's look at several examples of the heart condition of a woman who is considering separation or divorce.

A Cold Heart. You've been hurt, disappointed, and shamed. Maybe you don't even care about your marriage anymore. To protect yourself and maintain the appearance of routine and normalcy, you have allowed your heart to grow cold.

A Starving Heart. Your heart is shriveled, dehydrated, and shrunken due to lack of care, attention, and affection. You've tried to tell him how you feel, but you get a blank stare in return. Or worse, he pats you on the head and says, "Every marriage has problems. You're making too much of this."

A Bitter Heart. Because of sarcasm or constant arguing, your heart has built up scar tissue. Maybe you dish out cutting words yourself. Or perhaps you've become antagonistic in an effort to get even. You always want the last word—anything to win the argument.

A Divided Heart. You've sectioned off part of your heart and have begun to fantasize about a different life, a different marriage, a different man.

It is important to remind you again at this point that if you are in a marriage where the physical or emotional safety of you or your children is in jeopardy, you must remove yourself and your children from your home immediately. This book is not for you.

No matter what your heart looks and feels like right now, there is hope. I wrote in my prayer journal:

> *My heart's desire is to see scarred marriages healed (the scar tissue and excess baggage to be taken away). Teach them, Lord, to do it your way.*

When I was thinking of separating during my first marriage, my pastor's wife asked me to make a list of all the things I wanted to see change in my husband. That was the easy part. I easily ticked off a laundry list! Then she asked me "Now, what if he *never* changes?" Of course, you are not responsible for all the changes that must take place in order for your marriage to be restored, but change can begin with you.

It's Not About Him

This book is about a journey of discovery that will allow you to move from a disappointing or unfulfilling marriage to a place where God will give you new hope and a new focus. We won't be looking at magic formulas for changing your husband because I can't tell you what or what not to do to transform him.

Whisper this prayer to your Heavenly Father:

> *Lord, let all bitterness, anger, confusion, chaos, rebellion, slander, and malice be put away. Help me be kind, tenderhearted, and forgiving. I pray for emotional balance and that I won't be tossed about by wrong attitudes or moodiness.*

Maybe you feel your husband has been dishonest with you or perhaps there is no communication between the two of you. Maybe he is overly critical of you or too judgmental. It could be that you've been arguing about the same issues for so long you can't imagine how to break the cycle short of leaving him.

Ask the Lord to help you overcome your anger and indignation.

> *Lord, let me see a miracle in my marriage. Help me create a climate of righteousness, grace, and mercy in my home. Help me*

overcome discouragement and disappointment. Help me give and receive forgiveness.

It's hard sometimes to remember what being in love felt like and why we married this person in the first place. We find ourselves in a place where we're focused on our hurts, the slights, and the stinging words that have damaged the love that was once fresh and new. There may be a total lack of care and consideration—the feeling of not even wanting to try to regain the deep longings, close friendship, and caring companionship we once knew.

Unfortunately, you don't get to choose how your husband acts or feels. But you can go to the Lord and ask Him to help you take your eyes off yourself, your husband, your circumstances, and your troubles. The Lord can soften your heart and give you a teachable, willing spirit.

Second Cor. 4:8-9 says: "We are hard pressed on every side, but not crushed; perplexed, but not in despair; persecuted, but not abandoned; struck down, but not destroyed" (NIV).

Are these the thoughts and longings of your heart? Are these the words you pray? Can you even think of praying for yourself and your marriage right now? If not, I understand. Believe me, I've been there.

It's hard to look at where you are and what your marriage has become. There are strong emotions of anger, bitterness, loneliness, and isolation—the feeling that no one could possibly understand what you're dealing with. But God does.

A Picture of Clinging to God

As I prayed for the couples who came to the Weekend to Remember marriage conference sponsored by FamilyLife, God sometimes gave me a picture of what some of the women were experiencing in their marriages. Here's one of the pictures the Lord showed me:

> *The picture of clinging to God on a rocky, high place above the crashing waves. A stronghold for the oppressed—a picture of crawling up into God's arms for safety and protection—even as the storm rages.*

Maybe you're feeling angry at God for the condition of your marriage. Remember, God is the Great Physician who can work in you to change your heart, your life, and your marriage. Spend time with Him and allow Him to overrule your emotions as you are still before Him.

If you didn't have an earthly father with godly characteristics to run to and trust in, it may be hard to stop, be still, and listen for

God's whisper. Rest assured that God wants to tell you that you *are* loved, honored, and cherished—even if you aren't experiencing that in your marriage right now.

My dad abandoned me, and I felt my stepfather was distant and unaffectionate. I didn't understand how to ask for what I needed in my first marriage, so when I felt my needs weren't being met, I wasn't willing to stick around and wait for things to change. In my second marriage, I still have a hard time accepting and receiving the love and attention my husband, Dayne, shows me. I'm becoming aware of my tendency to withdraw, isolate myself, and feel unworthy. But with God's help, I look to my Heavenly Father to soothe those fears so I can freely accept the love, attention, and affection I truly want and need.

Maybe you haven't cried in months, even though you have felt desperately unhappy for a long time. Right now, the Holy Spirit is kneeling before you and quietly saying "I'm here—I want to come beside you and begin to help you look to the Father for the things you long for in your life." It's OK to cry and mourn the condition of your marriage today.

And then, when you are able, lay aside

your feelings and begin to consider doing some or all of the following:

1. Ask God to show you the condition of your heart and to give you a word or a picture that describes your feelings right now. Be willing to look honestly at your attitude with a genuine perspective of understanding how you really feel—even if it seems ugly, unloving, or sinful.

2. Look back through this chapter to find and write down one or more passages that touched you. When you find something that captures where you are right now, make it a prayer—an offering to God. Even if it's just one word.

3. Consider keeping a journal. This is a suggestion I will repeat throughout the book, especially later as we begin to look at praying Scripture. Right now the idea of putting your thoughts and feelings in writing may seem out of the question. I have found, though, that as I write things down, I can put them aside and trust that God sees and hears my cries and my prayers. I close the journal knowing that my problem or

concern is no longer in my hands, but in God's. Just consider it.

4. Allow yourself to see a glimpse of what God can do for your marriage and allow yourself to be just a little hopeful that He can bring resolution and reconciliation to your marriage.

God wants to help you find hope and restoration. He loves you and wants to give you hope and a future. That is a paraphrase of the passage from Jer. 29:11 that has been my "life verse" for many years now.

When I was discouraged and without hope that God saw my pain and heard my cries for my marriage, He brought this verse to mind to remind me that He does have a plan that is full of hope, as He does for you—even if you can't see it yet.

Scripture Meditations

"The revelation of GOD is whole and pulls our lives together. The signposts of GOD are clear and point out the right road. The life-maps of GOD are right, showing the way to joy. The directions of GOD are plain and easy on the eyes" (Ps. 19:7-8).

"From the four corners of the earth people are coming to their senses, are running back to GOD. Long-lost families are falling on their faces before him. GOD has taken charge; from now on he has the last word" (22:27-28).

"Love and Truth meet in the street, Right Living and Whole Living embrace and kiss! Truth sprouts green from the ground, Right Living pours down from the skies! Oh yes! GOD gives Goodness and Beauty; our land responds with Bounty and Blessing. Right Living strides out before him, and clears a path for his passage" (85:10-13).

"My theme song is God's love and justice, and I'm singing it right to you, GOD. I'm finding my way down the road of right living, but how long before you show up? I'm doing the very best I can, and I'm doing it at home, where it counts. I refuse to take a second look at corrupting people and degrading things" (101:1-3).

My Journal

_____

_____

_____

_____

_____

_____

_____

_____

_____

_____

_____

_____

_____

_____

_____

_____

_____

_____

_____

_____

_____

_____

_____

_____

_____

_____

_____

_____

_____

_____

_____

_____

_____

_____

_____

_____

_____

_____

_____

ACCOUNTABILITY

When I separated from my first husband and moved out of our family home, Travis was 10, Ryan was 6, and Jamie was 2.

I felt confident that I was a good mother. I taught natural childbirth, breast-fed each child, and made homemade baby food. I was able to stay home with both boys and worked only two days a week after Jamie was born. The kids and I went to church, and I was involved in Bible studies. I was a busy young mom who loved the Lord and adored her children.

Because my husband worked the graveyard shift for the last five years of our marriage, I felt like a single parent. I bathed and put the kids to bed each night and then spent the rest of the evening alone. I got them ready for school and daycare each morning and went to their school awards ceremonies and class plays by myself.

As a toddler, Travis had severe asthma. He spent many long hospital stays in an oxygen tent attached to an IV. When Travis was

4 years old and I was 9½ months pregnant with Ryan, Travis was hospitalized for five days with asthma. The pediatric nurses worried I would go into labor while I stayed with him at the hospital. I felt lonely and afraid. I was convinced my husband was not concerned about the well-being of me or my children and could be with us if he really wanted to. Travis came home from the hospital on Saturday and Ryan was born Sunday. Even though I stayed in the marriage until Jamie was two years old, I think that period was the lowest point.

My loneliest New Year's was when I had been separated from my husband for about six months and lived in small guest quarters. The kids were with me most of the time, but not this December 31. I went out with some friends from work to a party at a local college, but I welcomed the New Year alone.

Later that night I found my purse had been stolen. My house keys and car keys were in my purse, so I ended up sleeping on my girlfriend's couch in my party dress. I had wanted to be free of my marriage, but I was learning that what I thought I wanted— my freedom—came at a price. I missed my kids, my home, and the familiarity (as in family) of my prior life.

I also learned that it's not about me. If

you have children, they will be affected by your decision to separate and divorce. Once again, I am talking to the woman who is not in a marriage that is dangerous to her or her children. That calls for measures to remove yourself and your children from the situation immediately.

But there was no abuse in my home. My first husband and I didn't fight—our lives scarcely touched. I just became frustrated and gave up and decided we needed a physical separation. I was stubborn and determined. I felt I had spent enough time, read enough books, hoped, prayed, cried, and tried to get through to him long enough.

Because I was lonely and felt isolated in my marriage for many years and was physically separated from my husband for more than two years before the divorce was final, I rationalized that there was so little contact in our marriage relationship that the kids would go through the process unscathed. I was wrong. My second son and I have little contact, and my daughter, Jamie, told me once that she resented never knowing what it was like to live in one house with both parents. Talk about stabs to the heart! These are just a few glimpses of the legacy left by my choosing to divorce.

Dr. James Dobson of Focus on the Family answered the question about the impact of divorce on kids this way: "It's now known that emotional development in children is directly related to the presence of warm, nurturing, sustained, and continuous interaction with both parents. Anything that interferes with the vital relationship with either mother or father can have lasting consequences for the child."[1]

One landmark study revealed that 90 percent of children from divorced homes suffer from an acute sense of shock when the separation occurs, including profound grieving and irrational fears. Fifty percent report feeling rejected and abandoned. Indeed, half of the fathers were remiss in spending time with their children three years after the divorce. One-third of the boys and girls feared abandonment by the remaining parent, and 66 percent reported yearning for the absent parent with an intensity that researchers described as overwhelming. Most significant, 37 percent of the children were even unhappier and dissatisfied five years after the divorce than they had been 18 months following the divorce. In other words, time did not heal their wounds.[2]

Dr. Dobson closes his comments this way:

> That's the real meaning of divorce. It is certainly what I think about, with righteous indignation, when I see infidelity and marital deceit portrayed on television as some kind of exciting game for two.
>
> The bottom line is that you are right to consider the welfare of your children in deciding whether or not to seek a divorce. As empty as the marital relationship can be, it is likely that your kids will fare better if you choose to stick it out.[3]

Harvard sociologist Armand Nicholi III concluded, "Divorce is not a solution, but an exchange of problems."[4] Novelist Pat Conroy said of his own marriage breakup, "Each divorce is the death of a small civilization."[5] A woman wrote after her divorce, "Our divorce has been the most painful, horrid, ulcer-producing, agonizing event you can imagine. . . . I wish I could put on this piece of paper a picture of what divorce feels like. Maybe my picture would stop people before it's too late."[6]

My second marriage has been different. Dayne and I feel as though we're joined at the hip. We've had a close, loving, and affectionate relationship for 17 years. We've also had disappointments, challenges, and difficulties that include raising a blended family. We have faced severe financial crises and spiritual strongholds that we brought into our marriage. We both dragged excess baggage from our prior relationships into our marriage relationship.

As I wrote in my prayer journal, God dealt with my marriage and with me. What I wrote was painful and raw. But as God answered my prayers and the longings of my heart, I was able to discard many of the feelings I wrote about. God gave me new insights and healed longstanding strongholds. My hope is that women who read this book will see their lives, choices, and decisions as defining moments that can result in either unpleasant consequences or dreamed-of blessings. My prayer is that if you and your children are not victims of abuse and do not live in a situation that will result in emotional damage to you or to them, that you will examine and reconsider your thoughts of separation and divorce.

In stark contrast to my first marriage, rather than giving up or giving in—with God's help—I fought for my marriage to Dayne. We were determined to resolve our differences, and the enemy threw everything he could at us to try to discourage, frustrate, and cause division in our marriage.

So what are some ways to shape your anger, resentment, and hurt into positive steps to save your marriage?

Resist the Urge to Bad-Mouth Your Husband

Be careful about what you say and to whom you say it. Sincerely seeking advice and counsel from trusted friends or advisers and gossiping about your husband's irritating habits are two different things. First of all, determine in your heart that you will not gossip or vent to anyone about your husband strictly for the purpose of letting others know what a pain he is. The rules about gossip apply to marriage as well as to your circle of friends.

It is never a good idea to portray your husband as a tyrant. If he is truly a tyrant, then you should be removing yourself from the situation.

Remember, you're going to be praying for changes in your marriage relationship, and if you point out to anyone who will listen all your husband's shortcomings, it's going to be difficult for those you gossiped about him with to see him in a new light. If you've already fallen into this pattern, promise yourself you will stop it now.

Think about what he was like when the two of you dated and were first married. He may have exhibited some of the habits and tendencies early in your relationship that you find intolerable now, and you married him thinking you could change him. That is not to say he's free of the responsibility to contribute in a positive way to the restoration of your marriage, but realizing you chose to overlook these tendencies at one time rather than address them may help you extend grace now. Pray for people to come into his life who will influence him away from the behaviors that negatively affect your relationship with him. Pray that God will give you insight into ways you can appropriately respond to your husband's shortcomings. Do you pout, ignore, or give him the cold shoulder in hopes that he will miraculously realize what he's doing wrong and make the necessary changes? Or do you confront the problem at hand in a loving way that lets him know what you need from him? In other words, what is the attitude of your heart?

Marrying is a bit like entering college, imagining great times, parties, and laughter—and then realizing that you actually have to go to class and study.[7] A fulfilling marriage relationship is a lifelong study of your spouse, getting to know and understand who and what he is and is *not*. You may be telling others about his wrong attitudes and bad habits that God hasn't dealt with yet, but God is able to change him over time.

Bad-mouthing your husband is a thing completely different from seeking wise counsel and advice for restoring your marriage. Just be wise and careful when sharing about your husband and your relationship with him. Seek someone to talk to who will keep your confidences. A journal is extremely helpful for writing your feelings and frustrations—and a journal won't blab to others, judge, or hold a grudge against your husband later on.

Move Toward Resolution, Reconciliation, and Restoration

I do not counsel women to seek separation except in cases where the woman or her children are the victims of verbal, emotional, or physical abuse or where other extreme circumstances exist in the home, such as drug or alcohol abuse. My goal is to encourage women toward resolution, reconciliation, and restoration.

Don't Leave Your Family's Home

It is important that neither you nor

your husband move out of the home. Unless there's been abuse, you need to stay together under one roof. I understand that can be difficult when you feel you can hardly stand to be around him and don't really even like him—never mind any thoughts of love, care, or concern. But that's where the attitude you harbor in your heart comes in.

Once you are physically separated, it is practically inevitable that you will begin to process the *idea* of divorce. Let's say you set up two households. That becomes a financial hardship, which may already be one of your struggles. You arrange visitation schedules, creating fear and stress for your children. Physical separation increases the likelihood that one or both of you will begin relationships with another member of the opposite sex. Your heart becomes divided.

Seek Godly Counsel and Accountability

Find a godly woman with whom you can share your hurts. At the same time, seek her counsel and accountability. Being accountable to another woman means having someone you can be honest and transparent with, not just someone to have a pity party with. There were several women who wanted to provide Christian counsel and hold me accountable during my first marriage, but I shut them out. Find a friend who will pray with you and encourage you to seek God and restore your marriage. If possible, find a biblical Christian counselor who supports your goal of restoring your marriage. Even if your husband doesn't feel counseling is necessary, it can give you the support you need.

If you're not part of a church family, I encourage you to find a church or women's Bible study to be a part of. Not so you can vent, but as a place in a spiritual setting that will support the restoration of your marriage.

A Biblical View of Rebuilding and Restoration

Nehemiah 4 is a picture of rebuilding and restoration. The walls were crumbling around the city of Jerusalem—which can also be a picture of a failing marriage—crumbling and in ruins. Verses 13 and 14 say:

So I stationed armed guards at the most vulnerable places of the wall and assigned people by families with their swords, lances, and bows. After looking things over, I stood up and spoke to the nobles, officials, and everyone else: "Don't be afraid of them. Put your minds on the Master, great and awesome, and then fight for your brothers, your sons, your daughters, your wives, and your homes."

Lord, I will not be afraid. I will remember that you are great and awesome. You will frustrate the plans of the enemy and my husband's and my shortcomings.

What are the vulnerable places in your marriage?

How has the enemy caused hurt, pain, and division in your marriage?

Questions for Reflection

1. Are you willing to trust God and make a commitment to stay with your husband in your family home and begin to seek the road to finding God's will for your marriage?

2. Will you resolve to move toward resolution, reconciliation, and restoration of your marriage rather than moving toward separation and divorce?

3. Will you agree not to share embarrassing or negative information about your husband just so others will know what a pain he is?

4. Will you seek the advice of godly

friends and counselors on positive steps you and your husband can take to solidify your marriage?

5. If you're able to journal, begin to write down your decisions and choices, such as: "I choose to stay committed to my marriage and not physically separate from my husband and children. As difficult as this may be for me, with God's help, I choose to move toward resolution, reconciliation, and restoration of my marriage instead of moving toward separation and divorce."

Making a decision to change the direction of your marriage from separation and divorce to restoration and reconciliation requires a change of heart. Maybe you're not there yet. I challenge you to continue reading, journaling, praying, and trusting God.

Scripture Meditations

"How can a young person live a clean life? By carefully reading the map of your Word. I'm single-minded in pursuit of you; don't let me miss the road signs you've posted. I've banked your promises in the vault of my heart so I won't sin myself bankrupt" (Ps. 119:9-11).

"Be generous with me and I'll live a full life; not for a minute will I take my eyes off your road. Open my eyes so I can see what you show me of your miracle-wonders. I'm a stranger in these parts; give me clear directions" (vv. 17-19).

"Barricade the road that goes Nowhere; grace me with your clear revelation. I choose the true road to Somewhere, I post your road signs at every curve and corner. I grasp and cling to whatever you tell me; GOD, don't let me down! I'll run the course you lay out for me if you'll just show me how. Guide me down the road of your commandments; I love traveling this freeway!" (vv. 29-32, 35).

"Before I learned to answer you, I wandered all over the place, but now I'm in step with your Word" (v. 67).

"I watch my step, avoiding the ditches and ruts of evil so I can spend all my time keeping your Word. I never make detours from the route you laid out; you gave me such good directions" (vv. 101-102).

"By your words I can see where I'm going; they throw a beam of light on my dark path. I've committed myself and I'll never turn back from living by your righteous order" (vv. 105-106).

"Don't you see that children are GOD's

best gift? the fruit of the womb his generous legacy? Like a warrior's fistful of arrows are the children of a vigorous youth. Oh, how blessed are you parents, with your quivers full of children! Your enemies don't stand a chance against you; you'll sweep them right off your doorstep" (127:3-5).

My Journal

_____

_____

_____

_____

_____

_____

_____

_____

_____

_____

_____

_____

_____

_____

_____

_____

_____

_____

_____

_____

_____

_____

_____

_____

_____

_____

_____

_____

_____

_____

_____

_____

_____

_____

_____

_____

_____

_____

_____

_____

_____

_____

_____

_____

_____

_____

_____

_____

_____

_____

_____

_____

_____

_____

_____

_____

EXPECTATIONS, DISCONTENT, AND UNCONDITIONAL LOVE

What I share in this chapter is intended for women who are discouraged, frustrated, lonely, and feeling isolated. You may be angry and disappointed with your husband because of neglect, inattention, and a lack of affection. You'll know as you read if what I share is meant for you.

If there are added stressors on your marriage—such as infidelity, addiction to pornography, alcohol or drug use or gambling, clinical depression or chemical imbalance, or childhood sexual abuse—some of these suggestions may be helpful. But achieving a healthy marriage will require more than following the advice found on these pages. If you or your husband are dealing with these issues, it is imperative that you seek professional medical and psychological help.

My husband, Dayne, and I have gone for Christian counseling several times during our marriage. There's no shame in that, and for the problems many married couples face, it is essential. So be assured, there are no instant answers or quick cures for addictions, mental illness, or childhood sexual abuse issues. God knows your circumstances. If you are dealing with issues such as these, you need the expertise of a professional who can guide you on keeping yourself safe and point you to support groups or medical intervention.

In his book *Straight Talk,* Dr. James Dobson relates the story of a woman who is desperately unhappy in her marriage. Early in their marriage, although they struggled with financial problems, she and her husband were deeply in love and committed to one another. But then, as he began to receive promotions at work and worked longer hours, he came home tired and didn't feel much like talking. She had eaten dinner earlier with the kids, so she fixed him something to eat, and then he went to the phone and made business calls. On Saturdays, if he didn't work, he played golf with business associates. She became lonely, and things went downhill from there. There was no warmth or closeness, their sex life suffered, and she felt trapped and wanted to call it quits.[1]

Can you relate to this woman? Are parts of her story familiar? There may be variations—you may work outside the home and resent the fact that in addition to your full-time job, you feel responsible for the major portion of the housework, cooking, laundry, and child-care responsibilities. Your frustration is understandable, and you may well be asking yourself whether or not you want to continue in your marriage.

In the busyness of the world today, it's hard to stop and ask the hard questions. We just keep finding ourselves more and more drained—physically, mentally, emotionally, and spiritually. It's important to remember it's not *if* we will have struggles and conflict, but *how* we will handle them as they come.

We Are Powerless to Change Our Husbands

In her book *From Bondage to Bonding,* Nancy Groom writes:

The reality is that no amount of energy, no magic formula—nothing will bring about true change in another person. However, if we take the same energy and apply it to ourselves, God can do great things in our lives. First we have to really "get it"—down in our heart of hearts. We are powerless to change our husbands. Put simply, we must admit that the strategies we have used to change our husbands have not worked and that every attempt to change or control them will ultimately fail. Admitting we are powerless requires surrendering our husbands and our lives *completely* to God. It requires accepting . . . this is our reality. This doesn't sound like much of a solution, but it is the only solution that will calm our screaming fears and bring peace to our troubled hearts. We must surrender the obsession to try to change them because it is this obsession that blocks our emotional, intellectual, and spiritual growth.[2]

If we are preoccupied and engrossed in trying to change our husbands, our own emotional, mental, and spiritual well-being is affected.

Jesus Modeled a Balanced Life

In Marsha Means's book *Living with Your Husband's Secret Wars,* she writes,

As Christians, we often feel confused by the codependency concept. Jesus taught us to care for and about other people. He said, "Love your enemies, do good to those who hate you, bless those who curse you, pray for those who mistreat you" (Luke 6:27-28, NASB). The Epistles teach us to bear one another's burdens and to sacrifice for others. Does that mean that codependency is spiritual? Was Jesus codependent? I don't believe so. The Gospels show us a Jesus who wasn't afraid to say no, to speak the truth when He saw sinful behavior, and to take time out by himself and with friends. Jesus modeled a balanced way to live in relationships —He cared for others and He cared for himself.[3]

Jesus cared *for himself!* As women, wives, and mothers, we often take care of everyone else's needs before we even think about what *we* need. Knowing we have needs, why do we automatically expect our husbands to be the only ones to meet all those needs? We get caught up in thinking our husbands should provide for all our needs—materially, emotionally, romantically, and spiritually—and do all of it well!

When you first got married, did you really care about what you had and where you lived? Most of us started out in small apartments or houses with secondhand furniture, hand-me-down refrigerators, and cars we bought ourselves when we got our first job. Did we care that we didn't have it all? We had each other. We were in love and looked forward to the future knowing we could accomplish anything together. So what happened?

Gary Thomas, author of *Sacred Marriage,* said in the article "God's Design for Marriage," "We have to stop asking of marriage what God never designed it to give—perfect happiness, conflict-free living, and idolatrous obsession." He tells us that we can instead appreciate what God designed marriage to provide: partnership, spiritual intimacy, and the ability to pursue God—together.[4]

Soul Mate Versus Other-Centered

What does Thomas think is the most common misconception Christians have about marriage? "Finding a 'soul mate'— someone who will complete us," he says. "The problem with looking to another human to complete us is that, spiritually speaking, it's idolatry. We are to find our fulfillment and purpose in God . . . and if we expect our [husband] to be 'God' to us, he will fail every day. No person can live up to such expectations."[5]

God designed an *other-centered* union (in marriage) for a *me-centered* world—and that's a challenge!

Dealing with Unfulfilled Longings

Nancy Leigh DeMoss is a wonderful writer on women's issues. She writes about unfulfilled longings—those unsatisfied yearnings we may have at times:

All of us long for security and a certain level of creature comforts. Sometimes God is pleased to provide far more than we actually need. But sometimes He allows us to do without—to experience unfulfilled longings—so that we might come to recognize our need for Him.

The truth is, every human being has deep inner longings that will never be fulfilled this side of Heaven. Part of the purpose of those longings is to cause our hearts to become more attached to our true home in Heaven.

Those longings help us learn that true security cannot be found in people, things, or places. In fact, to look to anything or anyone other than Christ for fulfillment is to be insecure, because everything other than Him is subject to change or can be taken away.[6]

Can you begin to understand that you *will* have unmet needs and unfulfilled longings this side of heaven? God has brought together two imperfect people and longs to have them glorify Him within their marriage. Are you willing to be willing and allow God to begin to change your attitude as you look past your husband and all that he is—and isn't—and see God's plan for your marriage?

Real-Life Questions Concerning Unrealistic Dreams, Fantasies, and Wishes

Here are some practical, real-life questions to consider as you think about your marriage:

1. Do you read romance novels—including Christian ones—and dream about a more romantic life?

2. Do you watch soap operas and compare them to your own life and marriage?

3. Do you fantasize about your marriage and wish your husband could be more—more loving, more affectionate, more giving?

4. Do you compare your marriage to someone else's—wishing your husband could be more like your girlfriend's husband—or perhaps someone like your pastor?

5. Do you wish your husband made more money?

6. Do you think your husband should devote all his spare time and energy to making you happy and meeting all your wants, needs, and desires?

If you have unrealistic expectations of your husband and your marriage, you *will* be disappointed. Read that again. Say it to yourself. Now say it again out loud.

Giving and Loving Unconditionally

In his book *Starved for Affection,* author Randy Carlson describes four kinds of givers:

1. You give to get, also known as *manipulation*. The manipulative relationship has conditions attached and the flow of love can quickly be turned off when and if the manipulative person isn't getting his or her way.

2. You give if you get, also known as *withholding love* in order to exert control. The controller's goal is to stay in charge to get what he or she wants from the other person. (This is sometimes displayed in the sexual relationship.)

3. You don't give, but you expect to get anyway, which is pure selfishness.

4. You simply give, which is love.[7]

The Love Chapter

The Message, by Eugene H. Peterson, is a contemporary and straightforward paraphrase of the Bible from the original Greek and Hebrew languages. The following scripture, 1 Cor. 13:1-8, is taken from this version of the Bible and is commonly referred to as the love chapter:

If I speak with human eloquence and angelic ecstasy but don't love, I'm nothing but the creaking of a rusty gate.

If I speak God's Word with power, revealing all his mysteries and making everything plain as day, and if I have faith that says to a mountain, "Jump," and it jumps, but I don't love, I'm nothing.

If I give everything I own to the poor and even go to the stake to be burned as a martyr, but I don't love, I've gotten nowhere. So, no matter what I say, what I believe, and what I do, I'm bankrupt without love.

Love never gives up.

Love cares more for others than for self.

Love doesn't want what it doesn't have.

Love doesn't strut,
Doesn't have a swelled head,
Doesn't force itself on others,
Isn't always "me first,"
Doesn't fly off the handle,

Doesn't keep score of the sins of
others,
Doesn't revel when others grovel,
Takes pleasure in the flowering of
truth,
Puts up with anything,
Trusts God always,
Always looks for the best,
Never looks back,
But keeps going to the end.
Love never dies.

Unconditional Love

You can't change your husband. You
have no control over his behavior, moods,
and opinions, and it's unrealistic to think
that he will meet all of your wants, needs,
and desires. So what is a wife to do?

You can determine to respond to your
husband in a loving way unconditionally—
whether he deserves it, has *earned* it, or
even acknowledges your love and care.

My family will tell you that one of my
all-time favorite movies is *The Family Man*. It
is a story about glimpses and choices and
dreams coming true. At different times during the movie, the two main characters say
to each other "I choose us." Through everything we experience in our marriages, we
will have trials, discouragement, and disap-

pointments. However, we can learn, grow, and forgive, but most of all and through it all, we need to be able to say "I choose us."

The other day I came across our wedding invitation. There's a poem on the front of the invitation I want to share with you:

Love is friendship that has caught fire.
It is quiet understanding,
mutual confidence, sharing, and forgiving.
Love is content with the present,
hopes for the future,
and doesn't brood over the past.
If you have love in your life,
it can make up for a great many things you lack.
Without love, no matter what else there is,
it's not enough.

Remember when you first met? There was a friendship that somewhere along the line caught fire and became love—love that was content, hopeful, and didn't keep looking back to the past.

Lord, help me overcome the stumbling blocks and persevere. I can only look to you, Lord, depend on you, and trust you. Lord, you are sovereign—you rule over my time, my heart, my mind, and my schedule. Cause my heart and mind to turn to you. Cause my weary, frustrated, and broken heart to seek you and consciously desire you. As a mar-

riage partner, place in my heart the desire for a good and successful marriage.

Help me continually seek after your best in my life. Let my life and marriage mirror Jesus Christ, so that nothing in my life will bring dishonor or embarrassment to God. Help me live each moment seeking after your perfect will and desire for my life. Strengthen, renew, and invigorate my marriage.

Thank you, Lord. My heart is full of love and admiration for who you are. I know you love me and desire to show yourself in a mighty way in my heart and in my marriage. Thank you for what you've accomplished and still intend to do. I pray that my heart will be yielded to you and that you will release your power to heal my marriage.

Questions for Reflection

1. What are your goals for your marriage?

2. Are you expecting your husband to make you happy and give you all the love you need?

3. Are you willing to take your eyes off your husband and begin to look to God to fill, satisfy, meet your needs, and sustain you?

4. Can you begin to look at your husband through the eyes of love, with a pure heart, and be satisfied with who and what he is—and is not?

5. Will you refuse to allow your husband's behavior, moods, or opinions cause you to respond in an unkind, disrespectful, or controlling way?

Write down specific ways to show unconditional love to your husband.

Think of the four types of givers. Which one describes you? If there needs to be a change of heart, pray and ask God to help you become one who loves unconditionally.

If you read romance novels, watch soap operas, or use other fictional characters as the standard you expect your husband to match, will you give that up?

I hope you're beginning to notice a change in your attitude toward your husband. It may take time to heal old wounds, but God is trustworthy. I urge you to journal your thoughts, hurts, fears, and prayers as a way of cleansing the secret corners of your heart.

Scripture Meditations

"Post a guard at my mouth, GOD, set a watch at the door of my lips. Don't let me

so much as dream of evil or thoughtlessly fall into bad company. And these people who only do wrong—don't let them lure me with their sweet talk! May the Just One set me straight, may the Kind One correct me, don't let sin anoint my head" (Ps. 141:3-5).

"So now you can pick out what's true and fair, find all the good trails! Lady Wisdom will be your close friend, and Brother Knowledge your pleasant companion. Good Sense will scout ahead for danger, Insight will keep an eye out for you. They'll keep you from making wrong turns, or following the bad directions of those who are lost themselves and can't tell a trail from a tumbleweed. These losers who make a game of evil and throw parties to celebrate perversity, traveling paths that go nowhere, wandering in a maze of detours and dead ends" (Prov. 2:9-15).

"So—join the company of good men and women, keep your feet on the tried and true paths. It's the men who walk straight who will settle this land, the women with integrity who will last here" (2:20-21).

"Don't lose your grip on Love and Loyalty. Tie them around your neck; carve their initials on your heart. Earn a reputation for living well in God's eyes and the eyes of the people" (3:3-4).

"Dear friend, take my advice; it will add years to your life. I'm writing out clear directions to Wisdom Way, I'm drawing a map to Righteous Road. I don't want you ending up in blind alleys, or wasting time making wrong turns. Hold tight to good advice; don't relax your grip. Guard it well— your life is at stake! Don't take Wicked Bypass; don't so much as set foot on that road. Stay clear of it; give it a wide berth. Make a detour and be on your way" (4:10-15).

"Keep vigilant watch over your heart; *that's* where life starts. Don't talk out of both sides of your mouth; avoid careless banter, white lies, and gossip. Keep your eyes straight ahead; ignore all sideshow distractions. Watch your step, and the road will stretch out smooth before you. Look neither right nor left; leave evil in the dust" (vv. 23-27).

My Journal

_____

_____

_____

_____

_____

_____

_____

_____

_____

_____

_____

_____

_____

_____

_____

_____

_____

_____

_____

_____

_____

_____

_____

_____

_____

_____

_____

_____

_____

_____

_____

_____

_____

_____

_____

_____

_____

_____

THREE KEYS TO SURRENDER

Does anyone really like conflict? Unless you love to live in perpetual drama, you cherish the calm between the storms of life. The daily routine of life is much more peaceful when we're not fighting or trying to get even.

In my first marriage, there was no fighting; we rarely had a reason to argue. We simply lived in two separate worlds. My husband worked nights, and we allowed his work schedule to dictate the way we lived. He slept during the day. He had dinner with the children and me and went back to sleep at 7:30 P.M. in order to get up and go to work at 11 P.M. I made whatever decisions had to be made about the kids and the house. I slept alone during the week, and we didn't get on the same sleep schedule on the weekends. There was no conflict regarding intimacy—there just was none.

When Dayne and I got married, we had two different histories. I didn't know how to handle conflict—I didn't know what a fight was. My parents never fought. Dayne came from a background where just about everything was settled on a battleground. So when there was conflict, we both tended to withdraw. That was until I learned how to fight.

I developed a habit of saving up three issues—always three—and then blasted Dayne with my list. ". . . And another thing . . ." I always had to be right, and I always had to have the last word. Dayne usually listened and said nothing. Then, later, he might chance a comment, "So what you're saying is . . ." or try to do whatever was necessary to ease my irritation or frustration.

There's a comedian by the name of John Heffron. During his act, he talks about how women must go to school or a weekend camp or something to learn how to argue. He talks about "the tick"—that "tch, tch" sound women make. John says that's short-hand for what a jerk our husbands are. John says we ask our husbands a question and then answer it ourselves. "You know what your problem is? I'll *tell* you what your problem is!" For that reason, John says, our husbands don't even have to be there during an argument. He suggests we use our time management skills and have the fight in the car while running errands or on our way home from work. Then when we walk in the front door at the end of the day we can say, "Yep, won another one!"

That might be good for a laugh in a comedy routine, but if you're living with continual upheaval, antagonism, or hostility, it's not funny. I bring it up to get you thinking about the way you handle conflict. Recognizing our habits in dealing with conflict might help us develop tools to actually resolve conflict.

How does your husband react when you say those three little words? No, not "I love you" but "Can we talk?" Many men want to run for the hills. Dayne loves to sit and talk about things with me—unless I want to talk about a conflict. We're learning to avoid letting things build up or become a wall between us. I especially work to keep a clean slate with my husband so I don't end up blasting him with several problems or concerns at once.

We try to talk on the phone or by e-mail a couple of times during the day. I find e-mail works well for me if I have an issue I need to tell him about but I know he's going to need time to think about it. Then I wait until he's ready to talk. Sometimes I have to be patient for a day or two. I don't hit him with it when he first walks through the door at the end of the day.

In her book *Saying I Do Was the Easy Part: Secrets to a Dynamic and Fulfilling Mar-*

riage, Theda Hlavka lists 10 rules for good communication with your husband:

Rule No. 1: There will be no non-subjects—period. This is a subject that is understood to be off limits and not to be brought up under any circumstance. Nonsubjects between spouses are destructive. It takes two very mature people to handle painful subjects, but for the sake of the marriage, nonsubjects must become discussable subjects. Patience is the key. Don't give up until all subjects are open for discussion.

Rule No. 2: Whatever you say, say it with love (Eph. 4:15). The more difficult something is to hear, the more gently and tenderly it must be said. Honesty without gentleness is brutal. Make sure it needs to be said, then ask God to give you wisdom about what to say and when to say it.

Rule No. 3: Timing is everything. Don't try to talk about a difficult subject in the midst of chaos. Make a date to go to a quiet restaurant to talk. Don't start a hard conversation at bedtime.

Rule No. 4: Get to the point. Don't say more than you have to.

Rule No. 5: If he's not looking at you, he's probably not listening. If he's lost interest, get back to the point—or maybe you've said enough.

Rule No. 6: He can't read your mind. If you're not willing to say it out loud, let it go. Don't expect him to pick up your nonverbal hints.

Rule No. 7: Be as positive as possible. If you maintain a positive attitude generally, it is likely he'll be more willing to listen when you have a problem to discuss (Eph. 4:29).

Rule No. 8: Once you've shared your concerns, be quiet and listen. Don't react; just listen. That lets him know you are not attacking him and you value his input. James 1:19 says, "Everyone should be quick to listen, slow to speak and slow to become angry" (NIV).

Rule No. 9: When the time comes, be willing to accept correction from your husband. Don't be defensive when it's his turn to share his concerns in a non-threatening atmosphere.

Rule No. 10: Be forgiving. Colossians 3:13 tells us to "bear with each other and forgive whatever grievances you may have against one another. Forgive as the Lord forgave you" (NIV). It's a gift you give to one another.[1]

Communication is important when looking at our expectations about issues, concerns, and problems. Don't do what I used to do, which was blast my husband like the hot air from a fiery furnace when the door is opened!

Couples attending FamilyLife's Weekend to Remember marriage conference are asked to focus on the following:

1. One issue rather than many issues
2. The problem rather than the person
3. Behavior rather than character
4. Specifics rather than generalizations
5. Expression of feelings rather than judgment of character
6. "I" statements rather than "you" statements
7. Observation of facts rather than judgment of motive
8. Mutual understanding rather than who's winning or losing[2]

Both husband and wife should be willing to admit "I was wrong," say "I'm sorry," express regret, and be willing to ask for forgiveness. That involves both parties being in agreement, and your marriage may not be there right now. But if an issue surfaces, *you* can be the one to follow these principles in resolving conflict. Be willing to admit you were wrong (if you truly were wrong), say you're sorry (if you were the offending party), acknowledge any hurt you may have caused, and ask for forgiveness. Think of the positive effect that will have on your husband and your marriage relationship.

Giving Up the Right to Be Right

You may be thinking, *But I'm right!* I understand that it's hard when there's a conflict to stand back and look objectively at your husband's point of view.

Sometimes, though, it requires active listening to really hear what your husband is saying. If he's just ranting, that's one thing. But if he has a point, and you're choosing not to listen or consider his side, you may need to stop being stubborn and pay attention to what he's saying. You may have to choose to *give up the right to be right*.

There is often more than one way to resolve an issue. Dayne and I may have completely different perspectives—but that doesn't mean one viewpoint is right and the other is wrong. When you feel you're at an impasse, ask yourself, *Is this the hill I want to die on?*

How Can I Resolve Conflict Well in My Marriage?
Dennis and Barbara Rainey

Few couples like to admit it, but conflict is common to all marriages. We have had our share of conflict, and some of our disagreements have not been pretty. We could probably write a book on what not to do!

Start with two selfish people with different backgrounds and personalities. Now add some bad habits and interesting idiosyncrasies, throw in a bunch of expectations, and then turn up the heat a little with the daily trials of life. Guess what? You are bound to have conflict. It's unavoidable.

Since every marriage has its tensions, it isn't a question of avoiding them; it's a question of how you deal with them.

Resolving conflict requires knowing, accepting, and adjusting to your differences. One reason we have conflict in marriage is that opposites attract. It's strange, but that's part of the reason why you married who you did. Your spouse added a variety, spice, and difference to your life that it didn't have before.

But after being married for a while (sometimes a short while), the attractions become repellents. You may argue over small irritations—such as how to properly squeeze a tube of toothpaste—or over major philosophical differences in handling finances or raising children. You may find that your backgrounds and your personalities are so different that you wonder how and why God placed you together in the first place.

It's important to understand these differences and then to accept and adjust to them. Just as Adam accepted God's gift of Eve, you are called to accept His gift to you. God gave you a spouse who completes you in ways you haven't even learned yet.

Resolving conflict requires defeating selfishness. All of our differences are magnified in marriage because they feed what is often the biggest source of our conflict—our selfish, sinful nature.

Maintaining harmony in marriage has been difficult since Adam and Eve. Two people beginning their marriage together and trying to go their own selfish, separate ways can never hope to experience the oneness of marriage as God intended. The prophet Isaiah portrayed the problem accurately more than 2,500 years ago when he described basic human selfishness like this: "All of us like sheep have gone astray, each of us has turned to his own way" (Isa. 53:6 [NASB]). We are all self-centered; we all instinctively look out for number one, and this leads directly to conflict. As James 4:1-2 (NIV) says, "What causes fights and quarrels among you? Don't they come from your desires that battle within you? You want something but don't get it. You kill and covet, but you cannot have what you want. You quarrel and fight. You do not have, because you do not ask God."

This is the heart of what makes our conflict ugly. Our sin and selfishness focuses us on our own agenda like the sharpshooter who with the crosshairs of his rifle finds a target. Left to our own devices, we will go for what we think is important—every single time. And, as you might imagine, when two spouses are focused only on what they want, there is no real hope for peace . . . only the real expectation that things will get worse.

The answer for ending selfishness is found in Jesus and His teachings. He showed us that instead of wanting to be first, we must be willing to be last. Instead of wanting to be served, we must serve. Instead of trying to save our lives, we must lose them. We must love our spouses as much as we love ourselves. In short, if we want to defeat selfishness, we must give up, give in, and give all.

To experience oneness, you must give up your will for the will of another. But to do this, you must first give up your will to Christ, and then you will find it possible to give up your will for that of your mate. [3]

Romans 12:18 (NIV) says, "If it is possible, as far as it depends on you, live at peace with everyone." The longer I live, the more I realize how difficult those words are for many couples. Living peaceably means pursuing peace. It means taking the initiative to resolve a difficult conflict rather than waiting for the other person to take the first step.

Pursuing the resolution of conflict requires setting aside your own hurt, anger, bitterness, and not losing heart. Resolve that you will remain in solid fellowship daily with your husband—as well as with your children, parents, coworkers, and friends. Don't give the enemy ground by isolating yourself from someone you care about.

Resolving conflict often requires loving confrontation. Confronting your spouse with grace and tactfulness requires wisdom, patience, and humility.

The Power of the Tongue—Blessing and Cursing

Your ability to overcome destructive thoughts, words, and actions is determined in part by how you respond to conflict. The words you use are crucial. James 3:7-10 says "This is scary: You can tame a tiger, but you can't tame a tongue—it's never been done. The tongue runs wild, a wanton killer. With our tongues we bless God our Father; with the same tongues we curse the very men and women he made in his image. Curses and blessings out of the same mouth!"

One of the most important things Dayne and I learned from attending FamilyLife's Weekend to Remember marriage conferences was the concept of giving a blessing instead of an insult. During conflict and the ensuing arguments, things escalate quickly. I mentioned earlier my pattern of approaching Dayne with my concerns or grievances. I always had three issues—or would bring up issues from the past to make sure I had plenty of ammunition! You likely have a pattern to your arguments too. Would you believe me if I told you there is a sure-fire way to stop the escalation of an argument and diffuse it?

The next time an argument is about to

erupt, stop and think. *What's my pattern? Do I name-call? Do I bring up the past? Do I drag out a laundry list of grievances? Do I threaten divorce?* Whatever it is you typically do, do it differently this time. Once the issue is out on the table, if things begin to get heated, give a blessing instead!

You're probably thinking, *How do I do that?* I admit that early on Dayne was better at this than I was. I tended to keep things going and escalate the argument. I have learned to stop and remember that I don't have to be so angry and disagreeable when trying to resolve a conflict.

You know your husband and how best to diffuse the argument. The best approach for you might be to say, "You know, we always seem to have a disagreement about this same issue. Can we just sit down and calmly talk about it without yelling, name-calling, or threats?" Or you could offer to talk about it at a better time. Think of ways you can offer a blessing rather than falling into the same pattern where nothing gets resolved and the wounds just go deeper.

Lord, give me ideas of ways I can give a blessing in place of an insult. Help me remain committed to casting aside bitter, longstanding, unresolved conflict in my marriage.

The Lord gave me a picture of actually picking up a physical item to place in the middle of the living room floor to help me visualize that the item represents the problem—not me or my husband.

Another idea that's shared during the Weekend to Remember marriage conference is to look at each other and say, "You are not my enemy." That is hard to remember sometimes.

Cursing and Blessing
by Ney Bailey

I once had one of those terribly difficult relationships—on a scale of 1 to 10 it was about minus 20. It was in the deep freeze. If you could have put a stethoscope to my heart to reveal my words, you would have heard me saying, "I wish this person had never been born. This person makes my life miserable."

As I thought about this person, the words of James 3:9-10 (NIV) came to my mind. "With the tongue we praise our Lord and Father, and with it we curse men, who have been made in God's likeness. Out of the same mouth come praise and cursing. My brothers, this should not be."

In this passage the word "curse" means to speak evil of, or to not speak well of. The word "bless" means to speak well of.

I realized that I was cursing this person in my heart. It never occurred to me to bless this person—that thought went against every natural urge within me.

But it was obvious that the relationship wasn't improving through my own efforts. I began to pray that God would bless this person, and I determined that I would speak well of this person in my heart and to other people. I didn't feel like it, but I chose with my will to do what God's Word said.

To heal a relationship, someone has to start giving a blessing instead of a curse. Over time that relationship slowly began to heal, and today, on that same scale of 1 to 10, this relationship is probably a 7 or 8.

We reap what we sow. If we sow blessings, we are going to reap blessings. If we sow cursings, we will reap cursings. I'd rather reap blessings, wouldn't you?[4]

Wrong Thinking

We've looked at giving up the right to be right, giving a blessing instead of an insult, and our heart attitude—and how that affects our feelings and what we think. One of my favorite authors is Martha Peace. She's written a wonderful book titled *The Excellent Wife*. I've had the opportunity to read and study what Martha shares in her book, and I think it's one of the most intensive and comprehensive studies I've seen regarding the role of wife.

Martha talks about wrong thinking. She includes real-life examples of how our thinking can be wrong and can result in bitterness when we've been hurt. She provides examples of ways to change our thinking from bitter, ugly thoughts to kind, tenderhearted, and forgiving thoughts. Here are a few examples:

Bitter Thoughts

1. He doesn't love me—he only loves himself.
2. I will never forgive him.
3. I'll show him what it's like.
4. I hate him.

Kind, Tenderhearted, Forgiving Thoughts

1. He does not show love as he should,

but his capacity to love can grow (see Col. 3:14).

2. After all that the Lord has forgiven me for, this is the least I can do (see Matt. 18:32-33).

3. I'll give him a blessing instead (see 1 Pet. 3:9).

4. I can show love to him whether or not I feel like it (see 1 Cor. 13:4-7).[5]

Lies Women Believe

In her book *Lies Women Believe,* Nancy Leigh DeMoss outlines several lies many women believe and then shares the truth as found in God's Word.

Lie: God is not really good.

Truth: God is good, and everything He does is good. God doesn't make mistakes.

Lie: God doesn't love me.

Truth: God's love for me is infinite and unconditional. I don't have to perform to earn God's love or favor. God always has my best interests at heart.

Lie: God is just like my father.

Truth: God is exactly what He has revealed himself to be in His Word. God is infinitely more wise and loving than any earthly father could ever be.

Lie: God is not really enough.

Truth: God is enough. If I have Him, I have all I need.

Lie: God's ways are too restrictive.

Truth: God's ways are best. God's restrictions are always for my good. Resisting or rebelling against God's ways brings conflict and heartache.

Lie: God should fix my problems.

Truth: Life is hard. God is more concerned about glorifying himself and changing me than about solving my problems. God has an eternal purpose He is fulfilling in the midst of my problems. God wants to use my problems as part of His sanctifying process in my life. No matter what problem I am facing, God's grace is sufficient for me.

Lie: I'm not worth anything.

Truth: My value is not determined by what others think of me or what I think of myself. My value is determined by how God views me. To God, my soul is worth more than the price of the whole world. If I am a child of God, I am God's cherished possession and treasure.

Lie: I can't help the way I am.

Truth: If I am a child of God, I can choose to obey God. I am responsible for my own choices. I can be changed through the power of God's Spirit.

Lie: I have my rights.

Truth: Claiming rights will put me in bondage. Yielding rights will set me free.

Lie: I should not have to live with unfulfilled longings.

Truth: I will always have unfulfilled longings this side of heaven. The deepest longings of my heart cannot be filled by any created person or thing. If I will accept them, unfulfilled longings will increase my longing for God and for heaven.

Lie: I can sin and get away with it.

Truth: The choices I make today will have consequences; I will reap what I sow. Sin's pleasures only last for a season. Sin exacts a devastating toll. There are no exceptions. If I play with fire, I will get burned. I will not escape the consequences of my sin.

Lie: My sin isn't really that bad.

Truth: Every act of sin is an act of rebellion against God. No sin is small.

Lie: God can't forgive what I have done.

Truth: The blood of Jesus is sufficient to cover any and every sin I have committed. There is no sin too great for God to forgive. God's grace is greater than the greatest sin anyone could ever commit.

Lie: I am not fully responsible for my actions and reactions.

Truth: God does not hold me accountable for the actions of others. I am responsible for my own choices.

Lie: I cannot walk in consistent victory over sin.

Truth: If I am a child of God, I don't have to sin. I am not a slave to sin. Through Christ, I have been set free from sin. By God's grace and through the finished work of Christ on the cross, I can experience victory over sin.

Lie: I don't have time to do everything I'm supposed to do.

Truth: There is time in every day to do everything that God wants me to do.

Lie: I can make it without consistent time in the Word and prayer.

Truth: It is impossible for me to be the woman God wants me to be apart from spending consistent time cultivating a relationship with Him in the Word and prayer.

Lie: It is my responsibility to change my husband.

Truth: A godly life and prayer are a wife's two greatest means of influencing her husband's life. It is far more effective for a woman to appeal to the Lord to change her husband than to try to exert pressure on him directly.

Lie: I can't control my emotions.

Truth: I do not have to be controlled by my emotions. I can choose to fix my mind on the Truth, to take every thought captive to the Truth, and to let God control my emotions.

Lie: I can't help how I respond when my hormones are out of whack. (It's understandable to act like a shrew at certain times.)

Truth: By God's grace, I can choose to obey Him regardless of how I feel. There is no excuse for ungodly attitudes, responses, or behavior. My physical and emotional cycles and seasons are under the control of the One who made me, cares for me, and has made provision for each stage of my life.

Lie: If my circumstances were different, I would be different.

Truth: My circumstances do not make me what I am; they merely reveal what I am. If I am not content with my present circumstances, I am not likely to be happy in any other set of circumstances. I may not be able to control my circumstances, but my circumstances do not have to control me.

Lie: I just can't take any more.

Truth: Whatever my circumstance, whatever my situation, His grace is sufficient for me. God will never place more on me than He will give me grace to bear.

Lie: It's all about me.

Truth: All things were created by Him and for Him. It's all about God in the beginning and ending and center of all things. Him![6]

Lord, help me stand against fear, discouragement, and insecurity. Help me remember that You are in control. Let Your wisdom and power shine in my life. Perfect me with Your refining fire. Build character and strength into my life. Lord, forgive my stubborn pride and unyielding spirit. Help me look deep into my own heart instead of automatically assessing blame elsewhere.

Questions for Reflection

1. Do you have a pattern of escalating arguments? Think about what that pattern looks like.

2. If your husband typically instigates your arguments and disagreements, how can you biblically respond by giving a blessing? Journal your thoughts.

3. Can you consciously give up the right to be right and trust God to bring about the best outcome to a situation? Pray and ask God to help you if you feel resistant.

4. Journal some examples of wrong thinking you have, such as bitter, critical, or judgmental thoughts about your husband. Write a corresponding kind, tender, or forgiving thought about him.

5. Read again the list of lies women believe, and think about the ones that touch your heart the most. What lies will you trade for truths

about for yourself, your husband, and your marriage?

6. Choose a truth each day and meditate on it, write it on a sticky note and put it on your mirror and memorize it to make it a heartfelt truth in your life. You *can* start believing the truth!

We're getting to the heart of the matter. My sharing with you has been quite a journey. I've recalled some long-forgotten memories, but it's been good to see how God has been so gracious, loving, and faithful to me along the way.

Scripture Meditations

"Here are six things GOD hates, and one more that he loathes with a passion: eyes that are arrogant, a tongue that lies, hands that murder the innocent, a heart that hatches evil plots, feet that race down a wicked track, a mouth that lies under oath, a troublemaker in the family" (Prov. 6:16-19).

"The path of right-living people is level. The Leveler evens the road for the right-living. We're in no hurry, GOD. We're content to linger in the path sign-posted with your decisions" (Isa. 26:7).

"There will be a highway called the Holy Road. No one rude or rebellious is permitted on this road. It's for GOD's people exclusively—impossible to get lost on this road. Not even fools can get lost on it. No lions on this road, no dangerous wild animals—nothing and no one dangerous or threatening. Only the redeemed will walk on it. The people GOD has ransomed will come back on this road. They'll sing as they make their way home to Zion, unfading halos of joy encircling their heads, welcomed home with gifts of joy and gladness as all sorrows and sighs scurry into the night" (35:8-10).

"Thunder in the desert! 'Prepare for GOD's arrival! Make the road straight and smooth, a highway fit for our God. Fill in the valleys, level off the hills, smooth out the ruts, clear out the rocks. Then GOD's bright glory will shine and everyone will see it. Yes. Just as GOD has said" (40:3-5).

My Journal

_____

_____

_____

_____

_____

_____

_____

_____

_____

_____

_____

_____

_____

_____

_____

_____

_____

_____

_____

_____

_____

_____

_____

_____

_____

_____

_____

_____

_____

_____

_____

_____

_____

_____

_____

_____

A NEW TWIST ON SUBMISSION

Marriage was God's idea.

My husband, Dayne, and I began volunteering with Family-Life's Weekend to Remember marriage conferences in 1997. The first year we helped in the resource center—the bookstore. Each year thereafter we took on more responsibility: visiting churches and meeting with pastors and church secretaries, speaking at churches about the upcoming conferences, and delivering conference materials to churches in our area.

In April 2000 we were asked to become city ministry directors for the Lake Tahoe and Reno conferences. That year there were two back-to-back weekend conferences at beautiful Lake Tahoe. During the first weekend, Alan and Theda Hlavka spoke. Although we thoroughly enjoyed being a part of previous conferences, this one felt different, maybe because we sensed added involvement and connection because we were facilitating and helping coordinate the conferences.

Alan and Theda were transparent and honest about their relationship, and I identified with Theda. She was a strong-willed woman who, like me, would attempt to control most aspects of her marriage if not for her relationship with God. Speaking to the couples at one point, her husband, Alan, related, "We spent 33 months in counseling trying to figure out why we didn't love each other." What an incredibly honest and revealing statement! And here they were, confidently sharing and encouraging more than 300 couples attending the conference.

A New Look at Submission

On Sunday morning of that weekend, the men and women met in separate sessions. Theda spoke to the women, and we gave her our full attention. She said that if she had not learned to control her urge to control her husband, Alan would not have been speaking at the conference.

She then told the women in the session her definition of submission. She said, "Submission is ducking out of the way so God can have a clear shot at your husband." At first that didn't seem biblical or very spiritual, but I believe it's a realistic and contemporary thought. My heart heard it loud and clear! The other women did, too, because there was spontaneous laughter and then applause.

You may be saying, "That's right, God. I want You to have a clear shot at my husband—hit him over the head with a cast iron frying pan!" But stop and consider this. The action plan here is not about your husband. It's about you.

As you think about ducking out of God's way, picture your position. You are dropping to your knees—head bowed, eyes closed, humbled before the Lord—placing your husband and your marriage in God's hands. By purposefully getting out of God's way, you're taking your hands off your husband so that you stop being the filter through which your husband hears God.

It means you can no longer play Holy Spirit in your husband's life. Giving God a clear shot at him means you are no longer responsible for what God wants and desires to do *directly* in your husband's life. What a *freeing* thought! You are bowing down, getting out of the way, and trusting God with your husband.

Theda has written a book titled *Saying I Do Was the Easy Part*. She says in her book that our first priority as wives is to submit to God with all our hearts, souls, and minds. Then we are to complete our husbands and "add our strength to theirs."[1] I love that statement. I can add my strength to my husband's strength!

Jesus Was Submitted to God

Look at Jesus—He humbled himself and submitted His will to the will of the Father. He didn't whine, complain, or demand. He and His Father had determined before the beginning of time that's the way it would be. Remember the scene in the Garden of Gethsemane from *The Passion of the Christ*? Even though Jesus knew what lay ahead, He still sought the Father and agonized over what must happen next—and He was on His knees.

Being a Helper, Completer, and Partner

You can determine with your husband the best ways to come alongside him in partnership, helping and completing him. It's not about making either of you less. It's about being part of something more.

I love it when my husband seeks my advice and counsel. He says he loves talking to me! However, if I always tried to have the last word, I know he would get tired of coming to me to talk things through. I've learned over time that I can give my opinion—and I usually have a completely different perspective or feeling than Dayne has— but I will finish my thought with, "That's what I think, but it's important that you agree." Because, you know what? It *is* important that we be in agreement.

What Does Submission Look Like in Your Marriage?

Think about your temperament and personality and those of your husband. Are you strong-willed like me? Are you married to an easy-going, quiet guy? Then you must guard against taking control of every situation, discussion, and decision. You may have to consciously sit back and wait for your husband to take on the responsibility of being involved in decision-making.

Or maybe you are both stubborn and each of you wants your own way in every area. Then the two of you have different challenges in deciding how you will deal with godly submission. You may have a lot of information to give your husband so he can see your side of things, but then once it's said, listen graciously to what he has to say before a decision is reached.

Maybe you are the quiet, steady spirit in your family. You must be sure to make your thoughts and feelings known. It is no more fair for you to refuse to say what you think and make him responsible for making all the decisions than it is for you to wrestle away from him every important decision and make it without his input.

My husband is a natural leader and likes to be in charge. When he became a Christian in 1994, his desire was to be the servant-leader of our home. That presented a lot of challenges to both of us. I had been a single mom for a number of years and wasn't willing to give up control in certain areas. We moved from Southern California to Nevada because of my job transfer, and for several years I was the primary bread-winner while Dayne got established in his current profession as a financial planner. I had been a Christian since I was 12, and Dayne was new in his Christian walk. I dragged my feet on recognizing his leader-ship abilities in our home.

Dayne was working for a company I was wary of—I didn't like the focus of some of the business training. To me, there seemed to be an emphasis on greed and ma-terialism. I wanted Dayne to leave the com-pany well before he decided it was time. I gave my input and let him know how I felt, but it was his final decision when he would step away. And I struggled sometimes with wanting things to go my way!

He's now an estate and retirement planner. Although some of his early training seemed negative and worldly, he learned good business development tools that he would not have benefited from if I had pushed him to leave on my timetable. God also taught Dayne about spiritual discernment and how not to be drawn into the world's view of success.

I was guilty of complaining to a friend about the possible consequences of Dayne's decision to stay with the company and whining about why the whole family (meaning me) had to suffer because of the consequences of him staying with the company.

God may allow your husband to do things differently than you would like. He may allow your husband to make a mistake or travel down a rabbit trail in order to accomplish His perfect will. If you step in and try to interfere, fix, or repair the situation, you may actually be frustrating God's plan. God may be trying to deal with your husband in an area such as pride or anger. Sometimes we wives need to step back, watch and wait, and see God work in our husbands' lives.

During the period of waiting for God to lead Dayne to make a job change, I learned patience and self-control. God just kept whispering, "Be still, and know that I am God."

There's a great song by Billy Gaines about the trials of life that uses the analogy of traveling across a deep and wide river to reach the other shore. He sings that on the other side of the trial he'll be a better man. Isn't that what we all want for our husbands—for them to be better men?

What Interferes with Submission?

It can be especially hard to learn to partner with our husbands if we have been accustomed to running our marriages without their input or if we have jobs outside our homes where we are in charge. Perhaps some of us have grown up learning not to trust the significant men in our lives because of fathers who abandoned us or who were distant and unaffectionate. These are areas I've overcome in my own life with God's help. And sometimes I'm still stubborn, and sometimes I still struggle.

But, over time, God is allowing healing and wholeness and is helping Dayne and me find the "fit" within our marriage where we can be each other's helper, partner, supporter, encourager, lover, confidant, and best friend.

Mutual Accountability

You may have heard the term *mutual accountability*. In marriage, that means that the husband and wife hold each other accountable. It's a good thing if you and your husband can ask each other the tough questions such as "How am I doing in serving you and meeting your needs?" But you and your husband are both accountable to God first.

Dayne knows he can talk to me about anything without feeling threatened or judged. I know the importance of being there for him to share with and confide in. I always try to be accepting and affirming of my husband. But it is not my responsibility to keep my husband in line.

That's not to say that we condone sin in our husbands' lives. We are to support, encourage, and build our husbands up so they make good, right, and godly choices. In a completely healthy marriage, that support and encouragement goes both ways.

As women who are ultimately accountable to God, we can pray for our husbands, *Lord, make him the man you want him to be and do whatever you need to do to bring him to the place you want him to be.* Then stand back and watch God work.

Understanding Your Husband
by Barbara Rainey
Cofounder of FamilyLife

The book of Proverbs is probably my favorite in the Bible because it contains such practical wisdom about everyday life. One of its main themes is the value of developing understanding. Consider each of these verses on understanding: Chapter 2, verse 2 tells us to incline our hearts to understanding.

A man [or woman] of understanding walks straight (15:21).

Understanding is a fountain of life to him who has it (16:22).

Notice that understanding is not an end in itself; it is a vehicle to wisdom and direction. A person of understanding views life and people with God's perspective. This enables you to feel for another person, to identify with his struggles and difficulties, and to know what to say and when to be silent. In the husband-wife relationship, your level of understanding often determines your level of acceptance. However, total understanding is not necessary in order to demonstrate the total acceptance that is crucial in building your husband's self-esteem.

I once talked at a FamilyLife marriage conference to more than a dozen women who were experiencing problems in their marriages. One woman resented her husband's schedule. Another disagreed with her husband regarding how to discipline their children. A third was a young woman whose husband was jealous of the time she spent with her sister.

My advice to these women was basically the same: Seek to understand why your husband is feeling or acting this way. Focus on him, not on the negative circumstances and how you are affected.

Also, give him your complete acceptance, even if you don't totally understand him. It may be necessary to ask God to help you accept your husband, because it may not be easy to live with your situation.

Why is acceptance so important to a man? Because without it, he will feel that you are pressuring him to become something he's not. With it, he will sense that you love him for who he is today and not for what you hope he will become.[2]

Ephesians 5:33 tells husbands to love their wives as they love themselves, and then wives are told to respect their husbands. Do you find it difficult to respect your husband?

Lord, help me as I strive for wisdom, common sense, and knowledge. Help me love my husband unconditionally. And help me understand that loving unconditionally does not mean that I become a doormat but that I speak the truth in love.

I pray that my husband's heart will be softened and that he will lovingly choose to place our marriage under God's authority and leadership.

Help me take my hands off my husband and rely on you to open his heart and mind. And I submit my heart and will to you.

Time, Energy, and Focus

What takes your time, energy, and focus away from investing in your husband? Your children, job, or even your ministry may cause you to put your husband on the back burner. After your relationship with God, your husband is your next ministry. That can be difficult, especially if you don't feel honored and esteemed in return. However, you are responsible for how you live your life before God.

The following is a paraphrase of Matt.

25:35-40. It really touched my heart; see what you think:

I was hungry for breakfast, dinner,
and sometimes even lunch, snacks,
a kind word, a warm hug, to talk to you,
to be loved by you . . .
You gave me something to eat.
I was thirsty to feel accepted by you,
I mowed the lawn and needed
refreshing and . . .
You gave me something to drink.
I was a stranger; my mood was bad.
I had been unreasonable.
I had been mean, thoughtless, forgetful,
unhelpful, self-centered . . .
You invited me in.
I was naked; you did all my wash, even
when I dropped it on the floor.
You sewed on my missing buttons.
You ironed my wrinkled shirts.
You let me bare my soul to you.
You saw the real me that others never see—
With all my quirks and uncovered ugliness,
And you never exposed me before
our children, family, or friends . . .
You clothed me.
I was sick—you know my colds are
worse than anyone else's.
Sometimes I said things I didn't mean,

I got depressed and . . .
You cared for me.
I was in prison: My job got to me some days
and I withdrew from you.
When I was consumed with a problem,
when I was unforgiving,
When I didn't deserve anything
because of the way
I've treated you, and I was so ashamed . . .
You came to me.
Jesus would say to you,
"When you did these things for
your husband,
you did them for me."[3]

That is what I want to hear God say to me!

Questions for Reflection

1. Are you insisting on your own way? Is there a struggle for control in your home?

2. Consider the feelings you have about letting God deal with your husband. Are you willing to duck and get out of the way so God can have a clear shot at him?

3. Understand that your husband isn't perfect—and neither are you—but God wants you to have respect for your husband, even if you don't al-

ways agree with him or fully understand him.

4. Your first accountability is to God, and respecting your husband does not mean that you should follow him into sin. Speak the truth in love to your husband and then ask God to intervene; then trust God with the outcome.

5. Consider journaling your thoughts and prayers to God about how you can change your attitude and perspective on mutual accountability. You may look to God to give you the thoughts, words, and actions that will demonstrate your willingness to respect your husband and entrust him to God.

Scripture Meditations

"I know what I'm doing. I have it all planned out—plans to take care of you, not abandon you, plans to give you the future you hope for. When you call on me, when you come and pray to me, I'll listen. When you come looking for me, you'll find me. Yes, when you get serious about finding me and want it more than anything else, I'll make sure you won't be disappointed" (Jer. 29:11-13).

"If you want to live well, make sure you understand all of this. If you know what's good for you, you'll learn this inside and out. God's paths get you where you want to go. Right-living people walk them easily; wrong-living people are always tripping and stumbling" (Hos. 14:9).

"Don't pick on people, jump on their failures, criticize their faults—unless, of course, you want the same treatment. That critical spirit has a way of boomeranging. It's easy to see a smudge on your neighbor's face and be oblivious to the ugly sneer on your own. Do you have the nerve to say, 'Let me wash your face for you,' when your own face is distorted by contempt? It's this whole traveling road-show mentality all over again, playing a holier-than-thou part instead of just living your part. Wipe that ugly sneer off your own face, and you might be fit to offer a washcloth to your neighbor" (Matt. 7:1-5).

"Here is a simple, rule-of-thumb guide for behavior: Ask yourself what you want people to do for you, then grab the initiative and do it for *them*. Add up God's Law and Prophets and this is what you get" (v. 12).

My Journal

_____

_____

_____

_____

_____

_____

_____

_____

_____

_____

_____

_____

_____

_____

_____

_____

_____

_____

You've heard the old saying, "If Mama ain't happy, ain't nobody happy." That's because women typically set the mood and tone in our homes. But how do we set a positive tone when our lives and marriages are in turmoil?

When the marriage relationship isn't fulfilling, we may live in a sort of blue funk that colors our feelings and emotions. If those feelings aren't dealt with, we may pull away and become lonely and isolated, irritable, frustrated, and touchy.

One day, my friend Kim called me. She and her husband, Michael, were the city ministry directors with FamilyLife before Dayne and I assumed that responsibility. We were catching up on life when I mentioned I had been angry with Dayne for a couple of days and wasn't speaking to him. Kim asked, "So how much longer are you going to punish him?" I asked her what she meant by that. "Well, you say you've been mad at him for two days now. How much longer—12 hours, 24 hours—until you decide you've punished him enough?"

Her words hit me hard. I was arbitrarily giving Dayne the silent treatment to teach him a lesson. As I write this, I can't remember for the life of me what I was so angry about. Kim had a great point. Why do we feel we have to punish the people we're supposed to love and care about?

Can You Risk Being Married to an Imperfect Man?

Ask yourself this question: Are you willing to risk being married to and loving an imperfect man? Consider the alternatives. Some women go through several marriages and divorces seeking and searching for that perfect person. But they wreak havoc with the lives of those they toss aside in their quest for perfect love, complete happiness, and fulfilled contentment. They damage themselves and their children.

In his article "To the Wives of Busy and Unresponsive Men," James Dobson writes, "Many men . . . find it difficult to match the emotions of their wives. They cannot be what their women want them to be. But instead of looking at the *whole* man, assessing his many good qualities . . . the woman concentrates on the missing element and permits it to dominate their relationship. She's married to a good man, but he's not good enough!"[1]

So what are our choices? To be tossed about by our feelings and emotions, which we've learned we can't trust, or to step back and take a look at how we react and respond to our moods and emotions with regard to our husbands?

If you have begun to think of yourself as a victim or a martyr, it's time to change your perception. You married an imperfect man—bad habits, bad manners, bad hair (or no hair), and all. Guess what! He married an imperfect woman. You have both changed since your wedding day. In many ways, neither of you is the same as you were when you said your vows.

Conflicts, trials, and change aren't grounds for giving up and throwing away the years invested. It is possible to move through anxiety and frustration and choose to love this imperfect person. You can develop contentment and peace in the midst of your circumstances.

Apply the following verses and prayer to your marriage and family:

> Do you want to be counted wise, to build a reputation for wisdom? Here's what you do: Live well, live wisely, live humbly. It's the way you

live, not the way you talk, that counts. Mean-spirited ambition isn't wisdom. Boasting that you are wise isn't wisdom. Twisting the truth to make yourselves sound wise isn't wisdom. It's the furthest thing from wisdom—it's animal cunning, devilish conniving. Whenever you're trying to look better than others or get the better of others, things fall apart and everyone ends up at the others' throats.

Real wisdom, God's wisdom, begins with a holy life and is characterized by getting along with others. It is gentle and reasonable, overflowing with mercy and blessings, not hot one day and cold the next, not two-faced. You can develop a healthy, robust community that lives right with God and enjoy its results *only* if you do the hard work of getting along with each other, treating each other with dignity and honor *(James 3:13-18)*.

God's a safe-house for the battered, a sanctuary during bad times. The moment you arrive, you relax; you're never sorry you knocked *(Ps. 9:9-10)*.

Lord, break my heart and my husband's heart and bring us to a place of to-

tal surrender to you and your will. Soften our spirits. Lord, you are the key; we need Jesus and the power of the Holy Spirit. Help us look to you as our role model.

Determined Wives

I've met women over the years who have struggled with hurt, frustration, betrayal, disappointment, and discouragement. At some point during the testing and trials, I've observed their resolve—an unshakable, persistent decision and determination to trust the Lord with their husbands and their marriages. They were focused and committed.

I've been humbled and amazed as I watched God work in these women's lives! As He restored and renewed their marriages, they share their testimonies with other women. One of them told me that she learns something new in her marriage every day.

If you're willing to allow God to work in your life and in your marriage, He will give you strength, perseverance, and a wonderful testimony to the power of God.

I want to remind you here that I am not trying to convince you to stay in a marriage where there is physical violence, sexual abuse, serial affairs without true repentance, or addictions where you and your children are in danger. Your first priority is to keep yourself and your children safe.

God has given me a story that is bringing beauty from ashes, and I want to encourage you to seriously evaluate your feelings and emotions. There are women in my life who've watched Dayne and me struggle through many hardships and trials. Many of them have come to me to say they admire my strength and courage. But what they see isn't me—it's God working in me and in my life.

Ask God to give you a new determination and resolve to become an authentic woman of God—genuine and sincere. Ask Him to help you resist the urge to be manipulative, controlling, or ruled by emotion. Ask Him to help you be the same woman in your home with your husband and family as you are when the world is watching.

The trials and turmoils you face can be stepping-stones to a place of service to discouraged women. You will also be a living example to your husband and your children of the power of God and His faithfulness.

What Is Your Heart Set On?

In her book *The Excellent Wife,* Martha Peace provides a list of idols or false gods women may be drawn to: good health; physical appearance; a Christian marriage; being

treated fairly; a pain-free life; social ills
such as drug or alcohol abuse; a child or
children; another person; material things;
success; the approval of others; being in
control; having needs met.

Peace writes, "As long as things are going well in the areas you have your heart set
on, you will feel all right. When they do not
turn out as you desire, frustration and perhaps anxiety begin to build, even to the
point where you experience feelings of desperation. You become willing to do anything, including sin, to have your 'idol.'"[2]

She goes on to suggest that you set
your heart on knowing and obeying God's
Word, seeking Him and delighting in Him,
cultivating an attitude of joy and gratitude,
and glorifying Him in all you do.

What is your heart set on?

To Love Is to Risk

In *Living with Your Husband's Secret Wars*,
Martha Means writes,

> Relationships come with no guar-
> antees that our deepest longings for love
> and acceptance will be met. In fact, be-
> cause we live on a fallen planet, we can
> count on disappointment. Mutual inter-
> dependence is challenging at best; at
> worst, it remains unavailable or incredi-

bly painful. But to love is to risk. C.S. Lewis described this dilemma beautifully: 'To love at all is to be vulnerable. Love anything, and your heart will certainly be wrung and possibly be broken. If you want to make sure of keeping it intact, you must give your heart to no one, not even to an animal. Wrap it carefully round with hobbies and little luxuries, avoid all entanglements, lock it up safe in the casket or coffin of self-ishness. But in that casket—safe, dark, motionless, airless—it will change. It will not be broken; it will become un-breakable, impenetrable, irredeemable. The alternative to tragedy, or at least to the risk of tragedy, is damnation. The only place outside Heaven where you can be perfectly safe from all the dangers of love is Hell.'"[3]

Only you can decide if you're willing to take the risk of loving and being loved. There will undoubtedly be times of disappointment and discouragement, but the rewards are tremendous.

Striving and Persevering

Sometimes it's hard to see the difference between stubbornly striving and steadfastly persevering—following through or moving forward. Striving can become a stronghold where we allow our feelings and emotions to twist and bend with the wind. In our own strength, striving will cause us to strain and attempt to control.

By allowing God and the Holy Spirit to provide safekeeping over our feelings and emotions, God's perfect plan will be accomplished. Sometimes it's a gradual, deliberate process, but as we allow God to be our secure foundation, we can stand firm and persevere.

Practical Applications for Personal Contentment

You may be wondering, *But what about the practical application? Besides things such as seeking godly counsel, taking my eyes off my husband, and looking at submission in a new way, what are some practical steps I can take to help me hang in there?*

1. Find relaxing pursuits that help you rest and refocus. For me, that might be a pedicure, having lunch or a cup of tea or coffee with a friend, listening to a Christian radio station or a Christian CD, reading a daily devotional, taking a bubble bath, or browsing an antique shop.

2. If you have young children or grandchildren, take them on an ad-

venture. Go to a children's museum, the zoo, to a lake or the ocean, or a picnic at a local park. Watching children who are having fun has a way of renewing your perspective.

3. Look into Pilates, Jazzercise, or tap dancing. These are relaxing and renewing, not to mention good for your health. Or consider having a friend join you for a power walk or a prayer walk.

4. Take a class you will enjoy, such as photography, pottery, creative writing, painting, or quilting—something you've always been interested in. Having a creative outlet can help you enjoy a sense of accomplishment when you're struggling in other areas.

5. If your moods and emotions feel overwhelming, ask your doctor to check for a hormonal or chemical imbalance. Those can be treated with diet and/or medication.

Becoming a Woman of Purpose (Influence)

by Dennis and Barbara Rainey

When was the last time you thought about how you can grow in

Christ and make a difference for the Kingdom? Don't wait any longer. Now is the perfect time to step back and evaluate what your life looks like and to implement changes that can help you and your marriage grow stronger. There are four changes you can make to help you become a woman of purpose. These ideas won't cure every problem you have, but if you take each one seriously and commit to all four, positive change will take place in your home.

Pray for your husband every day. This is the most important investment you can make in your marriage. Prayer is one of the most intimate forms of communication God gives us. It knits your heart together with your husband's. Practically speaking, no other spiritual discipline does more toward placing the Lord at the center of your life and marriage. Prayer says, "You alone are Lord of my life. There is none other."

Never say the word *divorce*. Our society has become convinced that divorce is the cure for marital problems. It's not! There only two things that will mend your marriage—

hearts that are grounded in Christ and hard work. This year, commit to never saying the "D" word again.

Study your spouse. You may think you know your spouse, but have you really gotten to know him inside-out since you first got married? People change and so do their needs. In the next weeks and months, determine your mate's top three needs. Does he have an emotional need, a need for conversation, or a need for romance? Write down at least three ways you can demonstrate your love to your husband—then do them.

Have a personal daily quiet time. God gave us His Word to help us survive in a hostile world. As Ps. 119:105 says, "Your word is a lamp to my feet and a light for my path" (NIV). His Word is truth. If we are to experience change in our homes, we must admit we are lost and need to find our way to the truth of God's Word. I often hear Christians complain that the Bible can't be read in public schools. But are we faithfully reading it in our own homes? The Bible cannot light your path if it's lying unread on your bedside table.[4]

Questions for Reflection

1. Journal your thoughts about your feelings, emotions, and moods, paying special attention to your frustrations, fears, anxiety, unrealistic expectations, stubborn striving, and lies you have believed.

2. If you struggle with strong emotions during hormonal cycles, begin to chart those days on your calendar. When you are aware of hormonal changes that might make you less objective and more irritable, postpone major decisions and hard conversations.

3. What are things you enjoy doing that can help you refocus your time, talents, and energy toward activities that are relaxing, enjoyable, and just for you?

4. What does being an influencer mean to you? How can you positively influence others in your life?

5. What are some fun and relaxing things you can enjoy with your husband? Even if you don't think you'd be able to do them today, plan and dream for the future.

Scripture Meditations

"But you have God-blessed eyes—eyes that see! And God-blessed ears—ears that hear! A lot of people, prophets and humble believers among them, would have given anything to see what you are seeing, to hear what you are hearing, but never had the chance" (Matt. 13:16-17).

"The seed cast in the gravel—this is the person who hears and instantly responds with enthusiasm. But there is no soil of character, and so when the emotions wear off and some difficulty arrives, there is nothing to show for it. The seed cast in the weeds is the person who hears the kingdom news, but weeds of worry and illusions about getting more and wanting everything under the sun strangle what was heard, and nothing comes of it. The seed cast on good earth is the person who hears and takes in the News, and then produces a harvest beyond his wildest dreams" (vv. 20-23).

"And you continue, so bullheaded! Calluses on your hearts, flaps on your ears! Deliberately ignoring the Holy Spirit, you're just like your ancestors. Was there ever a prophet who didn't get the same treatment? Your ancestors killed anyone who dared talk about the coming of the Just One. And you've kept up the family tradition—traitors and murderers, all of you. You had God's Law handed to you by angels—gift-wrapped!—and you squandered it!" (Acts 7:51-53).

"There's nobody living right, not even one, nobody who knows the score, nobody alert for God. They've all taken the wrong turn; they've all wandered down blind alleys. No one's living right; I can't find a single one. Their throats are gaping graves, their tongues slick as mud slides. Every word they speak is tinged with poison. They open their mouths and pollute the air. They race for the honor of sinner-of-the-year, litter the land with heartbreak and ruin, don't know the first thing about living with others. They never give God the time of day" (Rom. 3:11-18).

My Journal

_____

_____

_____

_____

_____

_____

_____

_____

_____

_____

_____

_____

_____

_____

_____

_____

_____

_____

_____

_____

_____

_____

_____

_____

_____

_____

_____

_____

_____

_____

_____

_____

_____

_____

_____

_____

_____

_____

_____

_____

_____

_____

_____

_____

_____

_____

_____

_____

_____

_____

_____

_____

_____

_____

_____

_____

_____

PRAYING SCRIPTURE

Prayer is man giving God a foothold on the contested territory of this earth.—William Gurnell

Looking at the Spiritual Condition

I don't know your husband's spiritual condition. He may be completely unchurched. He may have been raised in church but now wants nothing to do with the things of God. Maybe he was a strong believer at one time but for some reason has been hurt or wounded and isn't walking with the Lord. Or maybe he feels his sin is preventing him from coming to the Lord. It could also be that he feels he's right where he needs to be spiritually, and he sees you as the problem.

God is able—no matter what spiritual condition you and your husband are in—to bring you both to the feet of Jesus and begin to restore, rebuild, and renew your marriage.

Why Pray Scripture?

If you're still stuck with feelings of frustration, anger, disappointment, and discouragement, you may feel that your prayers are ineffective. Praying Scripture will help keep your mind focused. Even if you don't feel like it, when you choose as an act of your will to begin the practice of praying Scripture, you will be honoring God and then your husband with your scriptural prayers. God will hear and see your heart attitude as you commit to praying Scripture for your husband, your marriage, and yourself.

A Pattern for Scriptural Prayers

What follows is an example of praying scripture taken from the first six verses of Ps. 1. Insert your husband's name in the blank. You can use any version of the Bible; these verses are taken from *The Message:*

"How well God must like
(_____)—
(_____) [doesn't] hang out at
Sin Saloon,
(_____) [doesn't] slink along
Dead-End Road,
(_____) [doesn't] go to Smart-
Mouth College.

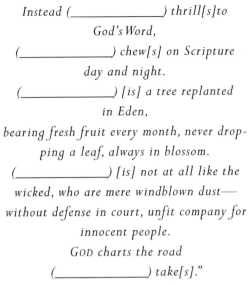

Instead (_____) thrill[s]to
God's Word,
(_____) chew[s] on Scripture
day and night.
(_____) [is] a tree replanted
in Eden,
bearing fresh fruit every month, never dropping a leaf, always in blossom.
(_____) [is] not at all like the
wicked, who are mere windblown dust—
without defense in court, unfit company for
innocent people.
GOD charts the road
(_____) take[s]."

This psalm lifts your husband up to God and asks God to bless him, keep him from walking or living in wicked company, with sinners, impostors, or untrustworthy men. Your prayer also asks God to cause your husband to delight and meditate on God and to be firmly planted by streams of water, the Living Water, Jesus. Finally, you are petitioning God to cause your husband to bear fruit, to not wither, and to prosper. Isn't that the prayer of our hearts for our husbands?

During the summer of 1996, I *lived* in the Psalms. By that I mean I wanted to pray for my husband's spiritual growth and maturity. Praying Scripture was the only way I

127

could see where I could keep my spiritual hands and eyes off Dayne and allow the Lord to grow my husband spiritually. The Psalms, Proverbs, Isaiah, Romans, Hebrews, and Ephesians are some of my favorite books of the Bible, full of scriptural prayers.

Here's one you can pray for yourself from Ps. 16:1-2, 5-8, 11:

> Keep me safe, O God, I've run for dear life to you. I say to GOD, "Be my Lord!" Without you, nothing makes sense. My choice is you, GOD, first and only. And now I find I'm your choice! You set me up with a house and yard. And then you made me your heir! The wise counsel GOD gives when I'm awake is confirmed by my sleeping heart. Day and night I'll stick with GOD; I've got a good thing going and I'm not letting go. . . . Now you've got my feet on the life path, all radiant from the shining on your face. Ever since you took my hand, I'm on the right way.

Let God show you how to pray Scripture for any and all of your hurts, worries, and concerns. As you are led to different chapters and verses, let the Lord show you how and what to pray from His Word.

Sometimes, maybe all you can do is sit quietly and meditate, and it may seem pointless and uneventful. But then a word or two, or possibly a song, might come to mind. Be willing to be still and patient—having patient endurance in the midst of life's challenges.

FamilyLife has put together a wonderfully comprehensive outline to guide you in how to pray, give you hope and encouragement, and provide practical application. This outline *alone* can give you a focus and an emphasis for how to journal and pray for yourself, your husband, and your marriage.

Won Without a Word by FamilyLife

Are you frustrated and discouraged that your husband does not believe in Christ or has accepted the Lord at some time in his life but isn't walking and growing spiritually? Use these scriptures and practical tips as a daily reminder to have Christ-centered thoughts, motives, and actions as a wife of an unbelieving or spiritually passive husband. You will be encouraged that God sees your needs and hears your prayers.

Prayer

"Now to him who is able to do immeasurably more than all we ask or imagine, according to his power that is at work within us" (Eph. 3:20, NIV).

Pray for a hedge of protection from evil around your husband (see Job 1:10).

"I sought the LORD, and He answered me, and delivered me from all my fears" (Ps. 34:4, NASB).

"Pour out your heart before Him; God is a refuge for us" (62:8, NASB).

"For the eyes of the Lord are on the righteous and his ears are attentive to their prayer" (1 Pet. 3:12, NIV).

Ask God to help you find a mature, godly woman who is well grounded in God's Word, and ask her to meet with you weekly or twice a month for prayer.

"Create in me a clean heart, O God, and renew a steadfast spirit within me" (Ps. 51:10, NASB).

"But as for me, my prayer is to You, O LORD, at an acceptable time; O God, in the greatness of Your lovingkindness, answer me with Your saving truth" (69:13, NASB).

Pray Col. 1:9 for the one you love.

Pray—"Set a guard, O LORD, over my mouth; keep watch over the door of my lips" (Ps. 141:3, NASB).

Pray for God to make you the wife you should be (see Ps. 27:11).

Give your unmet expectations and dreams to the Lord in prayer. Don't let the world influence them (see Rom. 12:2).

Give thanks for the things that you and

your husband are in agreement on in your marriage and home.

Pray—"When my heart is faint; lead me to the rock that is higher than I" (Ps. 61:2).

"Pray that the eyes of your heart may be enlightened, so that you will know what is the hope of His calling, . . . what is the surpassing greatness of His power toward us who believe" (Eph. 1:18-19, NASB).

Hope and Encouragement

"Behold, I am the LORD, the God of all flesh; is anything too difficult for Me?" (Jer. 32:27, NASB).

"For the battle is the LORD's" (1 Sam. 17:47, NASB).

"'For I know the plans that I have for you,' declares the LORD, 'plans for welfare and not for calamity to give you a future and a hope'" (Jer. 29:11, NASB).

"For our struggle is not against flesh and blood, but against the rulers, against the powers, against the world forces of this darkness, against the spiritual forces of wickedness in the heavenly places" (Eph. 6:12, NASB).

"For I have learned to be content in whatever circumstances I am" (Phil. 4:11, NASB).

God is ruling over the circumstances in your life; trust in His sovereignty (see Dan. 4:35).

"I can do all things through Him who strengthens me" (Phil. 4:13, NASB).

"How blessed is everyone who fears the LORD, who walks in His ways. When you shall eat of the fruit of your hands, you will be happy and it will be well with you" (Ps. 128:1-2, NASB).

"My hope is from Him. He only is my rock and my salvation" (Ps. 62:5-6, NASB).

"None of those who wait for You will be ashamed" (Ps. 25:3, NASB).

"I would have despaired unless I had believed that I would see the goodness of the LORD in the land of the living. Wait for the LORD; be strong, and let your heart take courage" (Ps. 27:13-14, NASB).

"I know that you can do all things; no plan of yours can be thwarted" (Job 42:2, NIV).

"You were tired out by the length of your road, yet you did not say, 'It is hopeless.' You found renewed strength, therefore you did not faint" (Isa. 57:10, NASB).

"Hope does not disappoint, because the love of God has been poured out within our hearts through the Holy Spirit who was given to us" (Rom. 5:5, NASB).

"For He Himself knows our frame; He is mindful that we are but dust" (Ps. 103:14, NASB).

"Though the mountains be shaken and the hills be removed, yet my unfailing love for you will not be shaken nor my covenant of peace be removed" (Isa. 54:10, NIV).

"Christ in you, the hope of glory" (Col. 1:27, NASB).

"Faith is the assurance of things hoped for, the conviction of things not seen" (Heb. 11:1, NASB).

Remember

God is a God of hope, power, and strength.

He sees your heart, hears your cries.

Your husband is a gift from God even if you married him without asking God.

God refreshes us when we are weary (see Isa. 40:31).

You are called by God to be godly and to be a loving companion to your husband.

"May the God of hope fill you with all joy and peace as you trust in him, so that you may overflow with hope by the power of the Holy Spirit" (Rom. 15:13, NIV).

"Your faith and hope are in God" (1 Pet. 1:21, NASB).

"The LORD will accomplish what concerns me" (Ps. 138:8, NASB).

"God is our refuge and strength, a very present help in trouble" (Ps. 46:1, NASB).

"No one can come to Me, unless the Father who sent Me draws him" (John 6:44, NASB).

"For as high as the heavens are above the earth, so great is His lovingkindness toward those who fear Him" (Ps. 103:11, NASB).

"And we know that God causes all things to work together for good to those who love God, to those who are called according to His purpose" (Rom. 8:28, NASB).

Practical Application

"Live in harmony with one another; be sympathetic, love as brothers, be compassionate and humble" (1 Pet. 3:8, NASB).

"Not returning evil for evil, or insult for insult, but giving a blessing instead; for you were called for the very purpose that you might inherit a blessing" (1 Pet. 3:9, NASB).

"Won without a word . . . as they observe your chaste and respectful behavior" (1 Pet. 3:1-2, NASB).

"Your adornment . . . a gentle and quiet spirit, which is precious in the sight of God" (1 Pet. 3:3-4, NASB).

"Whoever would love life and see good

days must keep his tongue from evil and his lips from deceitful speech" (1 Pet. 3:10, NIV).

"Seek peace and pursue it" (1 Pet. 3:11, NASB).

"She brings him good, not harm, all the days of her life" (Prov. 31:12, NIV).

"When she speaks she has something worthwhile to say, and she always says it kindly" (Prov. 31:26, NASB).

"The woman to be admired and praised is the woman who lives in the Fear-of-GOD" (Prov. 31:30).

As you think about your husband today, remember what is true, honorable, right, pure, lovely, and of good repute—all those things that are praiseworthy and excellent (see Phil. 4:8).

Tell your husband what you admire about him and the things he does really well.

The enemy sends us negative thoughts and criticism. Refuse to entertain them (see 2 Cor. 10:5).

Respect is your husband's greatest need from you and is commanded by God.

Become involved in at least one of your husband's interests.

"Let us not judge one another anymore, but rather determine this—not to put an obstacle or stumbling block in a brother's way" (Rom. 14:13, NASB).

Let your children hear you praising your husband.

"Love . . . do good . . . expecting nothing in return; and your reward will be great" (Luke 6:35, NASB).

Love is intentional regardless of feelings.

Your thoughts determine your attitudes.

Reminisce about your favorite romantic times with your husband.

Live your faith quietly. Don't preach to your husband (see 1 Pet. 3:1).

By our speech we can ruin the world, turn harmony to chaos (see James 3:6).

Respecting your husband means appreciating, honoring, esteeming, admiring, and valuing him. Showing respect includes being polite, attentive, obliging, and accommodating.

"If possible, so far as it depends on you, be at peace with all men" (Rom. 12:18, NASB).

"So then we pursue the things which make for peace and the building up of one another" (Rom. 14:19, NASB).

"Esteem [your husband] very highly . . . because of [his] work" (1 Thess. 5:13, NASB).

"Do not seek revenge or bear a grudge against one of your people, but love your neighbor as yourself. I am the Lord" (Lev. 19:18, NIV).

"Never pay back evil for evil to anyone" (Rom. 12:17, NASB).

"A gentle answer turns away wrath" (Prov. 15:1, NASB).

"For the mouth speaks out of that which fills the heart" (Matt. 12:34, NASB).

"Let your speech always be with grace, as though seasoned with salt, so that you may know how you should respond to each person" (Col. 4:6, NASB).

A Christian wife bridles her tongue (see James 1:26).

Have realistic expectations of your spouse (see Rom. 8:7-8).

Pleasing your husband pleases God and gives you joy (see 1 Cor. 10:31-33).

Live your faith in an honest and natural way.

Make it your habit to love your husband with your actions. Start today.

Meeting your husband's and family's needs is your number one ministry. Don't overcommit yourself outside the home.

"Do not let any unwholesome talk come out of your mouths, but only what is helpful for building others up according to their needs, that it may benefit those who listen" (Eph. 4:29, NIV).

Can your husband trust his heart with you? Are you loyal? Can he say, "I have no lack of gain" because of you (see Prov. 31:11).

"Do nothing from selfishness or empty conceit, but with humility of mind regard one another as more important than yourselves" (Phil. 2:3).

FamilyLife web site:
http://www.familylife.com/articles/article_detail.asp?id=465

Prayer Power

Stormie O'Martian has written a series of books on the power of prayer. Below is a list of 30 different topics she suggests wives pray for their husbands.[1] For the next 30 days, take one subject each day, write that subject in your journal, and then write out a short prayer for your husband. Make it uplifting, caring, and godly. Ask God to do His will in your husband's life in this particular area of his life.

His Wife: Start by praying for change in yourself, and ask God to create in you a clean heart.
His Work
His Finances
His Sexuality

His Affection

His Temptations

His Mind

His Fears

His Purpose

His Choices

His Health

His Protection

His Trials

His Integrity

His Reputation

His Priorities

His Relationships

His Fatherhood

His Past

His Attitude

His Marriage: Pray for God's protection that no person or situation will ever be allowed to harm your marriage, and pray that a spirit of divorce will never enter into your marriage.

His Emotions

His Walk

His Talk

His Repentance

His Deliverance

His Obedience

His Self-Image

His Faith

His Future

Questions for Reflection

1. Can you see the benefits of journaling and praying Scripture? Have you been able to journal your thoughts, words, and prayers?
2. Will you commit to praying for your husband and your marriage?
3. Can you express your love and gratitude to God for His Word?
4. Encourage your children to pray for your family. God certainly hears the prayers of a child.

Scripture Meditations

"We find ourselves standing where we always hoped we might stand—out in the wide open spaces of God's grace and glory, standing tall and shouting our praise. There's more to come: We continue to shout our praise even when we're hemmed in with troubles, because we know how troubles can develop passionate patience in us, and how that patience in turn forges the tempered steel of virtue, keeping us alert for whatever God will do next. In alert expectancy such as this, we're never left feeling short-changed. Quite the contrary—we can't round up enough containers to hold everything God generously pours into our lives through the Holy Spirit!" (Rom. 5:2-5).

"So, my friends, this is something like what has taken place with you. When Christ died he took that entire rule-dominated way of life down with him and left it in the tomb, leaving you free to 'marry' a resurrection life and bear 'offspring' of faith for God. For as long as we lived that old way of life, doing whatever we felt we could get away with, sin was calling most of the shots as the old law code hemmed us in. And this made us all the more rebellious. In the end, all we had to show for it was miscarriages and stillbirths. But now that we're no longer shackled to that domineering mate of sin, and out from under all those oppressive regulations and fine print, we're free to live a new life in the freedom of God" (7:4-6).

"This resurrection life you received from God is not a timid, grave-tending life. It's adventurously expectant, greeting God with a childlike 'What's next, Papa?' God's Spirit touches our spirits and confirms who we really are. We know who he is, and we know who we are: Father and children. And we know we are going to get what's coming to us—an unbelievable inheritance! We go through exactly what Christ goes through. If we go through the hard times with him, then we're certainly going to go through the good times with him!" (8:15-17).

"Meanwhile, the moment we get tired in the waiting, God's Spirit is right alongside helping us along. If we don't know how or what to pray, it doesn't matter. He does our praying in and for us, making prayer out of our wordless sighs, our aching groans. He knows us far better than we know ourselves, knows our pregnant condition, and keeps us present before God. That's why we can be so sure that every detail in our lives of love for God is worked into something good" (vv. 26-28).

My Journal

_____

_____

_____

_____

_____

_____

_____

_____

_____

_____

_____

_____

_____

_____

_____

_____

_____

_____

_____

_____

_____

_____

_____

_____

_____

_____

_____

_____

_____

_____

_____

_____

_____

_____

_____

_____

_____

I am *not* a poet. But God uses poetry in my life to tell a story. This is a poem God gave me that is a picture of my life:

I see my life as a woven tapestry
   try
Full of rich color and texture.
There are places that are some-
   what worn and tattered
With dropped stitches and frayed
   edges
And when I look up from the backside
   of my life, sometimes I'm sad,
For I see only the flaws and failures,
   and the hurried rush to finish that
   portion.

But God sees me and my life from above.
Once again, He shows me the rich hues and
   intricate, delicate care
that He has taken to help fashion me and
   make me a priceless work of art,
A gift to everyone who knows me, even if I
   can't always see it.

Do you see only the worn, tattered places, dropped stitches and frayed edges, the flaws and failures and the hurried rush of your life?

Encouragement and Tools

I encourage you to rest and renew your heart, mind, and spirit. Throughout the book, I've tried to provide practical, biblical principles to encourage you. As I was thinking about rest and renewal, I asked myself, *Am I giving them too many things to do and too much to think about?* My hope and prayer is that you are well-equipped and encouraged in your journey, not bogged down or discouraged.

I've taken the tools my husband and I have learned and applied through our association with FamilyLife, included personal stories about marriage and divorce and helpful articles and excerpts from leading authorities on Christian marriage. I hope you will take these thoughts, ideas, and principles and begin to apply them as the Lord and your heart lead you.

Maybe you already have. There will be those who will grasp the concepts and take them to heart immediately and who may have already seen dramatic changes. My purpose in writing this book is for you to have a change of heart and turn from the cross-roads of separation and divorce.

Devotional Quiet Time and the Stuff of Life

I've had the opportunity to complete two Bible studies by Nancy Leigh DeMoss that have helped me learn to rest in the Lord. One is *A Place of Quiet Rest* and the other is *A 30-Day Walk with God in the Psalms*. Both have enriched my daily devotions.

However, I am not always as disciplined and consistent as I would like to be. The prayer journal I kept prior to FamilyLife's Weekend to Remember marriage conferences compelled me to pray, journal, and be still. However, at other times, I went days and sometimes weeks without a consistent devotional time. What I've found is that I lose my spiritual focus, and my relationship with God, my husband, and my family suffers.

You may be asking yourself how you can find time in your day to journal and pray. You may have to get creative. For most of the time I was consistently journaling, I was working between 60 and 80 hours each week as a real estate appraiser. I had my own business, and I knew if I didn't get up early each morning and have time with the Lord, the rest of my day would be filled with the stuff of life, and there would be no quiet time with God. Think about setting the alarm earlier to begin your day with journaling and prayer.

If that's not possible, are there small breaks in your day—before heading to work or before bed at night, on your lunch hour, or while waiting for the kids during gymnastics or soccer practice—where you could journal and pray?

In the fall of 2004 I typed my handwritten prayer journal into an outline. I was working at a job that was a challenge each day. I was at work at 7 A.M. and it took nearly an hour to get there. I escaped at lunchtime to a nearby park and read over the prayer journal outline and wrote my notes in a steno pad. That was my way to reconnect—my quiet time. That's just one suggestion as to how you can fit this practice into your day. It doesn't have to be an hour, or even a half-hour. If you have only 15 minutes a day, it can be enough to be still and allow God to speak to your heart and share your heart with Him.

Let Go of Perfection

I've discovered it's OK to be imperfect. You have a certain amount of energy, and you need to use it wisely. It's not necessary to completely exhaust yourself in order to please God. He just wants to know your heart is with Him. Let Him show you how to live. You may have regrets from the past and fears of the future that prevent you from a contented rest. Let go of yesterday and tomorrow, and ask God to show you what He has for you today.

Here is a Scripture prayer from Ps. 51:10-12:

Create in (_____) a pure heart, O God, and renew a steadfast spirit within (_____).

Do not cast (_____) from your presence or take your Holy Spirit from (_____).

Restore to (_____) the joy of your salvation, and grant (_____) a willing spirit, to sustain (_____).

That prayer takes only seconds, but it lifts you to God.

Finding Joy in the Journey

The Lord can and will move in your life and marriage, even if you only have a small amount of time each day. The prayer journal I kept spanned more than four years! The important thing is to find joy in the journey:

1. Allow your life—your past, present, and future—to be imperfect. Stop stubbornly striving in your own strength.

2. Allow yourself and your husband to be imperfect. That's why we need Jesus. Stop competing and start completing. Add your strength to your husband's and be united in the journey.

3. Meditate on the gifts of the Spirit:

   Love—affection for others (commitment and passion)

   Joy—exuberance for life (excitement and devotion)

   Peace—serenity (peacefulness and calm)

   Patience—willingness to stick with things (courage and composure)

   Kindness—a sense of compassion in the heart (sympathy and tenderness)

   Goodness—basic holiness sinks in (integrity and morality)

   Faithfulness—loyal commitments (fidelity and devotion)

   Gentleness—not needing to force your way in life (forgiveness and harmony)

> *Self-Control*—gathering and di-
> recting your energies wisely
> (dignity and self-discipline)
> (Adapted from Gal. 5:22-23.)

4. Reach a place of contented rest. In the midst of a tumultuous, upsetting, and frustrating relationship, pray that God will make you a still point in the midst of the chaos and fill you with all hope.

Roadblocks to Contented Rest

What keeps you from contented rest? *Weariness:* Do you feel like the more you do, more is expected of you? Does *woundedness* from your past keep you from rest? Or does *worry* about the future prevent you from resting? The weight of weariness, woundedness, and worry can wreck us. Ask God to share these burdens and allow Him to help you rest in Him, then trust Him to heal your wounds and soothe your worries.

A Proverb a Day

If time is your enemy, there's a way to have a quick study and develop wisdom. The Book of Proverbs contains 31 chapters—one for each day of the month. Keep a Bible with you, and when you have a moment in your day, go to the chapter of Proverbs that corresponds to the date on the calendar. Each time you read a Proverb, you'll gain wisdom and a new insight for daily living.

God Is at Work in a Thousand Different Ways

God is doing a thousand things in everything He does. As you move away from the crossroads of separation and divorce, you are moving toward reconciliation, restoration, and renewal—in your marriage and in your life. God is at work in you, your husband, and in your marriage in a thousand different ways.

Consider a Sabbath Rest

You probably have a very busy life right now. You may have young children, be working outside the home or home schooling, have active adolescents or teenagers or ministry obligations.

Consider a Sabbath rest. It may be on a Sunday (the Sabbath day) or any time you can pull away and just rest and relax. At our house we have a "jammie" or "veg" day (or sweats day—whatever you want to call it). We have a big breakfast, rent some movies, pop some popcorn, and just enjoy an afternoon away from the world. With our schedules we may accomplish this only every few months, but it's fun to look forward to that day of rest. That's our version of a Sabbath rest.

Questions for Reflection

1. How would you describe your life —do you have a picture? Remember it's an *unfinished* picture. God isn't finished with you, your husband, or your marriage yet.

2. Can you find some time in each day to spend alone with the Lord?

3. Do you think your family would benefit from a Sabbath rest day? Plan one.

4. How do you think your husband and children will respond if they see you stepping away from the busyness of life and having quiet time with the Lord?

5. If today is a blank page—a clean canvas—how can you use it in a way that is pleasing to the Lord?

This chapter is meant to be an encouragement—not to place more demands on you. Make a conscious choice to choose contented rest and renewal and to develop the fruit of the Spirit in your life.

Scripture Meditations

"Is there anyone around who can explain God? Anyone smart enough to tell him what to do? Anyone who has done him such a huge favor that God has to ask his advice? Everything comes from him, everything happens through him; everything ends up in him. Always glory! Always praise!" (Rom. 11:34-36).

"Love from the center of who you are; don't fake it. Run for dear life from evil; hold on for dear life to good. Be good friends who love deeply; practice playing second fiddle. Don't burn out; keep yourselves fueled and aflame. Be alert servants of the Master, cheerfully expectant. Don't quit in hard times; pray all the harder. Help needy Christians; be inventive in hospitality. Bless your enemies; no cursing under your breath. Laugh with your happy friends when they're happy; share tears when they're down. Get along with each other; don't be stuck-up. Make friends with nobodies; don't be the great somebody. Don't hit back; discover beauty in everyone. If you've got it in you, get along with everybody. Don't insist on getting even; that's not for you to do. 'I'll do the judging,' says God. 'I'll take care of it.' Our Scriptures tell us that if you see your enemy hungry, go buy that person lunch, or if he's thirsty, get him a drink. Your generosity will surprise him with goodness. Don't let evil get the best of you; get the best of evil by doing good" (Rom. 12:9-21).

"The world is unprincipled. It's dog-eat-dog out there! The world doesn't fight fair. But we don't live or fight our battles that way—never have and never will. The tools of our trade aren't for marketing or manipulation, but they are for demolishing that entire massively corrupt culture. We use our powerful God-tools for smashing warped philosophies, tearing down barriers erected against the truth of God, fitting every loose thought and emotion and impulse in the structure of life shaped by Christ. Our tools are ready at hand for clearing the ground of every obstruction and building lives of obedience into maturity" (2 Cor. 10:3-6).

My Journal

_____

_____

_____

_____

_____

_____

_____

_____

_____

_____

_____

_____

_____

_____

_____

_____

_____

during trials and testings, I remember that *boot camp* is making me stronger for my journey through life and into eternity.

A Family Reformation Must Begin with Individual Sacrifice
by Dennis Rainey

A family reformation must begin with individual sacrifice. But sacrifice takes courage. It takes courage to confess and repent of sin. It takes courage to keep your wedding vows and uphold your biblical roles in the family. It takes courage to raise godly children in the midst of a godless culture. When every voice around you screams, "Compromise! Surrender! Take the easy way out!" it takes courage to stand for the truth of God's Word.

Compromise represents a far greater risk than courage. As difficult as it is to stand for truth, it is much harder to live with the consequences of moral failure.

When every voice around you screams "Compromise! Surrender! Take the easy way out!"—when marriage is hard and parenting is harder, when your wedding vows could easily be broken, stand for the truth!

YOUR LEGACY

Walls
Their wedding picture mocked them
from the table,
These two whose minds no longer
touched each other.
They lived with such a heavy barricade
between them that
Neither battering ram of words nor artilleries of touch could break it down.
Somewhere, between the oldest child's first tooth
and the youngest daughter's graduation, they lost
each other.
Throughout the years, each slowly unraveled that
tangled ball of string called self,
And as they tugged at stubborn knots each hid
his searching from the other.
Sometimes she cried at night and begged the
whispering darkness
To tell her who she was.
He lay beside her, snoring like a hibernating
bear, unaware of her winter.
Once, after they had made love he wanted to tell
her how afraid he was of dying,

But fearing to show his naked soul, he spoke in-
stead about the beauty of her breasts.
She took a course in modern art,
trying to find herself in colors
splashed upon a canvas,
And complaining to other women
about the men who are insensitive.
He climbed into a tomb called "the office,"
wrapped his mind in a shroud of paper
Figures and buried himself in customers.
Slowly, the wall between them rose,
cemented by the mortar of indifference.
One day, reaching out to touch each other, they
found a barrier
They could not penetrate, and recoiling from the
coldness of the stone, each retreated from the
stranger on the other side.
For when love dies, it is not in a moment
of angry battle, nor when fiery bodies
lose their heat. It lies panting, exhausted, expir-
ing at the bottom of a wall
it could not scale.

Author Unknown

This is the sad legacy of a failed marriage. Is this how you'd like your legacy—
the future you leave to your children and
grandchildren—to read? There's nothing
worse than getting to the end of life and
having so many regrets.

Leaving a Godly Legacy

The final session of the Weekend to Remember marriage conference is called
"Leaving a Godly Legacy." For Dayne and
me, that means that beginning with us, we
won't carry the generational sins of our
families forward. Alcoholism, mental instability, infidelity, divorce, abandonment, and
desertion are part of our family's history.

Fortunately, we also have a godly heritage. Both of us had praying grandmothers
who knew the Lord and faithfully prayed for
their grandchildren. I believe those prayers
are what saved our lives and brought us to
the Lord. Both of us have had experiences
where our lives could have been snuffed out
in an instant, but the Lord protected and
preserved us. We have a great desire to glorify God and return the love, grace, and
protection He afforded us in keeping and redeeming our lives and marriage.

A pastor once asked us to think about
our purpose here on earth. What do we call
this journey of life? He compared it to boot
camp in the military. We learn how to live,
love, and fight the spiritual battles—all in
preparation for eternity. We also learn to
equip, encourage, and influence others
along the way in the journey. Many times

God will reward your faithfulness. And one more irreplaceable family will join the ranks of a family reformation![1]

Fourteen Values to Shape Your Family Culture
by Tim Stafford

God first. Honoring God comes before anything else.

Concern for others. Jesus told us to love our neighbors as we love ourselves. That means constantly and scrupulously paying attention to their welfare. Included in "concern for others" are concerns like evangelism and justice.

Hard work. Whatever work we do, we should do it wholeheartedly. We work not just to please ourselves but also to please God and all those to whom we are responsible.

Truthfulness. Our words should be filled with truth, and we should use no words that undercut the truth.

Generosity. God wants an overflowing and openhanded love for others, especially in how we invest our possessions.

Submission. In many different settings—work, marriage, church, government—we fit into a larger scheme and submit to the leadership of someone else. Submission implies accepting our limited role in the world.

Sexual fidelity. Faithfulness to a marriage partner implies eliminating anything that interferes with our love for that partner. Single people express sexual faithfulness by living chaste lives.

Family unity and love. The family is a core unit that demands respect, support, and love. So does the church, as God's family.

Boundaries. God has given each individual certain areas of responsibility that belong to him or her alone. First is his or her body. Next is his or her property. Jobs, family, and relationships may also be private. These areas of individual responsibility should be protected. Theft, sexual harassment, and gossip are some of the sins that violate these boundaries.

Joy and thanksgiving. Celebration should be part of every day, because we recognize all that God does for us.

Rest. We work within the limits of the time and ability God has given us. After working, we stop for renewal.

Care for creation. God made humans responsible to develop and care for all that He has created. Harmony, not destruction, should mark the interaction between human development and the rest of God's creation.

Contentment. With whatever we have and whatever we are, in whatever place or position God has put us, we should learn to be at peace.

Grace. We are meant to follow in the footsteps of God himself, offering forgiveness and grace to others even when it isn't deserved.[2]

There may have been generational sins —habits, addictions, divorce, desertion, or abandonment—in your family history. Will you resolve that the legacy you leave will be a godly one—serving the Lord in your marriage?

Questions for Reflection

1. Will you commit to leaving a godly legacy?

2. Will you take the challenges from "A Family Reformation" and "14 Values to Shape Your Family Culture" and let them be guideposts to reconciliation, restoration, and renewal in your marriage relationship?

3. If you haven't shared the contents of this book with your husband, will you begin by telling him what God is showing you in renewing your commitment to your husband and your marriage?

Scripture Meditations

"If we die with him, we'll live with him; if we stick it out with him, we'll rule with him; if we turn our backs on him, he'll turn his back on us; if we give up on him, he does not give up—for there's no way he can be false to himself" (2 Tim. 2:11-13).

"Stay on good terms with each other, held together by love. Be ready with a meal or a bed when it's needed. Why, some have extended hospitality to angels without ever knowing it! Regard prisoners as if you were in prison with them. Look on victims of abuse as if what happened to them had happened to you. Honor marriage, and guard the sacredness of sexual intimacy between wife and husband. God draws a firm line against casual and illicit sex. Don't be obsessed with getting more material things. Be relaxed with what you have. Since God assured us, 'I'll never let you down, never walk off and leave you,' we can boldly quote, God is there, ready to help, I'm fearless no matter what. Who or what can get to me? . . .

"Make sure you don't take things for granted and go slack in working for the common good; share what you have with others. God takes particular pleasure in acts of worship—a different kind of 'sacrifice'— that take place in kitchen and workplace and on the streets" (Heb. 13:1-6, 16).

My Journal

_____

_____

_____

_____

_____

_____

_____

_____

_____

_____

_____

_____

_____

_____

_____

_____

_____

_____

_____

_____

_____

_____

_____

_____

_____

_____

_____

_____

_____

_____

_____

_____

_____

_____

_____

_____

STARTING OVER

I Am Divorced
author unknown

I have lost my husband,
but I am not supposed to mourn.
I have lost my children;
they don't know to whom they belong.
I have lost my relatives; they do not ap-
*   prove.*
I have lost his relatives; they blame me.
I have lost my friends; they don't know how
*   to act.*
I feel I have lost my church.
Do they think I have sinned too much?
I'm afraid of the future. I'm ashamed of the
*   past.*
I'm confused about the present.
I'm so alone.
I feel so lost.
God, please stay by me.
You are all I have left.

I've shared with you some of the stories and consequences of my divorce. I've also told you how, with God's help, I fought for my second marriage. I'd like to give you a broader view of the ways God worked in my marriage with Dayne.

We came into our marriage with a lot of excess baggage—spiritual strongholds, and we both had sinned. Dayne was not a Christian when we got married May 6, 1989, and I certainly wasn't walking with the Lord. We had purchased a home together, and we had a garden wedding there with our four children from our previous marriages. Our son together, Garrett, was born in April of 1990.

We moved from Valencia, California, to Carson City, Nevada, in January of 1994—10 days after the Northridge earthquake. We felt like Lot and his wife leaving Sodom and Gomorrah—except I didn't look back!

On Easter Sunday 1994 Dayne became a Christian. His conversion was nothing short of miraculous and a total surprise to me. God often uses the element of surprise in my life because He knows me so well. If I had any idea that Dayne was close to accepting the Lord, I would have worried, wondered, tried to analyze, figure out, and generally tried to second-guess whatever plans God had for my husband.

During the next few years we suffered through many trials and adversities. God was growing us both up quickly, strengthening us. But there were lingering strongholds

YOUR LEGACY

Walls
Their wedding picture mocked them
from the table,
These two whose minds no longer
touched each other.
They lived with such a heavy barricade
between them that
Neither battering ram of words nor ar-
tilleries of touch could break it down.
Somewhere, between the oldest child's first tooth
and the youngest daughter's graduation, they lost
each other.
Throughout the years, each slowly unraveled that
tangled ball of string called self,
And as they tugged at stubborn knots each hid
his searching from the other.
Sometimes she cried at night and begged the
whispering darkness
To tell her who she was.
He lay beside her, snoring like a hibernating
bear, unaware of her winter.
Once, after they had made love he wanted to tell
her how afraid he was of dying,

But fearing to show his naked soul, he spoke in-
stead about the beauty of her breasts.
She took a course in modern art,
trying to find herself in colors
splashed upon a canvas,
And complaining to other women
about the men who are insensitive.
He climbed into a tomb called "the office,"
wrapped his mind in a shroud of paper
Figures and buried himself in customers.
Slowly, the wall between them rose,
cemented by the mortar of indifference.
One day, reaching out to touch each other, they
found a barrier
They could not penetrate, and recoiling from the
coldness of the stone, each retreated from the
stranger on the other side.
For when love dies, it is not in a moment
of angry battle, nor when fiery bodies
lose their heat. It lies panting, exhausted, expir-
ing at the bottom of a wall
it could not scale.
Author Unknown

This is the sad legacy of a failed marriage. Is this how you'd like your legacy—
the future you leave to your children and
grandchildren—to read? There's nothing
worse than getting to the end of life and
having so many regrets.

Leaving a Godly Legacy

The final session of the Weekend to Remember marriage conference is called "Leaving a Godly Legacy." For Dayne and me, that means that beginning with us, we won't carry the generational sins of our families forward. Alcoholism, mental instability, infidelity, divorce, abandonment, and desertion are part of our family's history.

Fortunately, we also have a godly heritage. Both of us had praying grandmothers who knew the Lord and faithfully prayed for their grandchildren. I believe those prayers are what saved our lives and brought us to the Lord. Both of us have had experiences where our lives could have been snuffed out in an instant, but the Lord protected and preserved us. We have a great desire to glorify God and return the love, grace, and protection He afforded us in keeping and redeeming our lives and marriage.

A pastor once asked us to think about our purpose here on earth. What do we call this journey of life? He compared it to boot camp in the military. We learn how to live, love, and fight the spiritual battles—all in preparation for eternity. We also learn to equip, encourage, and influence others along the way in the journey. Many times during trials and testings, I remember that *boot camp* is making me stronger for my journey through life and into eternity.

A Family Reformation Must Begin with Individual Sacrifice
by Dennis Rainey

A family reformation must begin with individual sacrifice. But sacrifice takes courage. It takes courage to confess and repent of sin. It takes courage to keep your wedding vows and uphold your biblical roles in the family. It takes courage to raise godly children in the midst of a godless culture. When every voice around you screams, "Compromise! Surrender! Take the easy way out!" it takes courage to stand for the truth of God's Word.

Compromise represents a far greater risk than courage. As difficult as it is to stand for truth, it is much harder to live with the consequences of moral failure.

When every voice around you screams "Compromise! Surrender! Take the easy way out!"—when marriage is hard and parenting is harder, when your wedding vows could easily be broken, stand for the truth!

God will reward your faithfulness. And one more irreplaceable family will join the ranks of a family reformation![1]

Fourteen Values to Shape Your Family Culture
by Tim Stafford

God first. Honoring God comes before anything else.

Concern for others. Jesus told us to love our neighbors as we love ourselves. That means constantly and scrupulously paying attention to their welfare. Included in "concern for others" are concerns like evangelism and justice.

Hard work. Whatever work we do, we should do it wholeheartedly. We work not just to please ourselves but also to please God and all those to whom we are responsible.

Truthfulness. Our words should be filled with truth, and we should use no words that undercut the truth.

Generosity. God wants an overflowing and openhanded love for others, especially in how we invest our possessions.

Submission. In many different settings—work, marriage, church, government—we fit into a larger scheme and submit to the leadership of someone else. Submission implies accepting our limited role in the world.

Sexual fidelity. Faithfulness to a marriage partner implies eliminating anything that interferes with our love for that partner. Single people express sexual faithfulness by living chaste lives.

Family unity and love. The family is a core unit that demands respect, support, and love. So does the church, as God's family.

Boundaries. God has given each individual certain areas of responsibility that belong to him or her alone. First is his or her body. Next is his or her property. Jobs, family, and relationships may also be private. These areas of individual responsibility should be protected. Theft, sexual harassment, and gossip are some of the sins that violate these boundaries.

Joy and thanksgiving. Celebration should be part of every day, because we recognize all that God does for us.

Rest. We work within the limits of the time and ability God has given us. After working, we stop for renewal.

Care for creation. God made humans responsible to develop and care for all that He has created. Harmony, not destruction, should mark the interaction between human development and the rest of God's creation.

Contentment. With whatever we have and whatever we are, in whatever place or position God has put us, we should learn to be at peace.

Grace. We are meant to follow in the footsteps of God himself, offering forgiveness and grace to others even when it isn't deserved.[2]

There may have been generational sins —habits, addictions, divorce, desertion, or abandonment—in your family history. Will you resolve that the legacy you leave will be a godly one—serving the Lord in your marriage?

Questions for Reflection

1. Will you commit to leaving a godly legacy?
2. Will you take the challenges from "A Family Reformation" and "14 Values to Shape Your Family Culture" and let them be guideposts to reconciliation, restoration, and renewal in your marriage relationship?

3. If you haven't shared the contents of this book with your husband, will you begin by telling him what God is showing you in renewing your commitment to your husband and your marriage?

Scripture Meditations

"If we die with him, we'll live with him; if we stick it out with him, we'll rule with him; if we turn our backs on him, he'll turn his back on us; if we give up on him, he does not give up—for there's no way he can be false to himself" (2 Tim. 2:11-13).

"Stay on good terms with each other, held together by love. Be ready with a meal or a bed when it's needed. Why, some have extended hospitality to angels without ever knowing it! Regard prisoners as if you were in prison with them. Look on victims of abuse as if what happened to them had happened to you. Honor marriage, and guard the sacredness of sexual intimacy between wife and husband. God draws a firm line against casual and illicit sex. Don't be obsessed with getting more material things. Be relaxed with what you have. Since God assured us, 'I'll never let you down, never walk off and leave you,' we can boldly quote, God is there, ready to help, I'm fearless no matter what. Who or what can get to me? . . .

"Make sure you don't take things for granted and go slack in working for the common good; share what you have with others. God takes particular pleasure in acts of worship—a different kind of 'sacrifice'—that take place in kitchen and workplace and on the streets" (Heb. 13:1-6, 16).

My Journal

_____

_____

_____

_____

_____

_____

_____

_____

_____

_____

_____

_____

_____

_____

_____

_____

_____

_____

_____

_____

_____

_____

_____

_____

_____

_____

_____

_____

_____

_____

_____

_____

_____

_____

_____

_____

STARTING OVER

I Am Divorced
author unknown

I have lost my husband,
but I am not supposed to mourn.
I have lost my children;
they don't know to whom they belong.
I have lost my relatives; they do not ap-
* prove.*
I have lost his relatives; they blame me.
I have lost my friends; they don't know how
* to act.*
I feel I have lost my church.
Do they think I have sinned too much?
I'm afraid of the future. I'm ashamed of the
* past.*
I'm confused about the present.
I'm so alone.
I feel so lost.
God, please stay by me.
You are all I have left.

I've shared with you some of the stories and consequences of my divorce. I've
also told you how, with God's help, I fought
for my second marriage. I'd like to give you
a broader view of the ways God worked in
my marriage with Dayne.

We came into our marriage with a lot of excess baggage—spiritual strongholds, and we both had sinned. Dayne was not a Christian when we got married May 6, 1989, and I certainly wasn't walking with the Lord. We had purchased a home together, and we had a garden wedding there with our four children from our previous marriages. Our son together, Garrett, was born in April of 1990.

We moved from Valencia, California, to Carson City, Nevada, in January of 1994— 10 days after the Northridge earthquake. We felt like Lot and his wife leaving Sodom and Gomorrah—except I didn't look back!

On Easter Sunday 1994 Dayne became a Christian. His conversion was nothing short of miraculous and a total surprise to me. God often uses the element of surprise in my life because He knows me so well. If I had any idea that Dayne was close to accepting the Lord, I would have worried, wondered, tried to analyze, figure out, and generally tried to second-guess whatever plans God had for my husband.

During the next few years we suffered through many trials and adversities. God was growing us both up quickly, strengthening us. But there were lingering strongholds that we had sought counseling for with several pastors on different occasions. But "the elephant in the living room" remained.

I could go into detail to give you an idea of how serious our situation was. But I'll just tell you that by 2000 we had problems that were insurmountable in our own strength.

We had reached an impasse when someone suggested a Christian counselor in our area.

The first time we met with Rick, we spent nearly two hours pouring our hearts out about the issues we had not been able to overcome. There was a lot of pent-up anger and frustration. At the end of the first session, Rick said, "I'm surprised you two aren't divorced." The issues that were suffocating our marriage were serious enough that we both knew they could not be resolved without God's help.

Rick met with us once a week for several weeks. The sessions were intense and difficult. But Rick was focused and determined, and we had God on our side. Rick brought it down to a simple drawing with a circle and stick figures—God, Dayne, and I were on the inside of the circle—everything else was on the outside. Of course, that's an oversimplification, but that was the bottom line.

Rick also gave us copies of a chapter from the book *Tough Talk to a Stubborn Spouse.*[1] There are 60 short chapters, each dealing with a different reason or complaint people use to justify divorce.

The author says that you should definitely put a miserable marriage out of its misery. But the way he suggests doing that is different from anything I've read on the subject.

His approach includes vows that you and your husband make to each other to end your disappointing marriage—sort of a private divorce. Then you make vows to one another to die to self. Finally, you remarry.

If your spouse is unwilling to exchange these vows with you, your hands are tied. Do your best to understand why he will not cooperate, and attempt to work out a compromise.

If your spouse is uncooperative, you can still make the second vow to God on your own. In fact, I highly recommend it.

If your spouse is willing to exchange these vows with you, be thankful.

When you read these vows for the first time, make sure you are alone and in a place that is free from distraction. Read through them with reverence and caution. Be sure that you take the time not only to grasp them mentally but also to emotionally grasp their implications.

Arrange a time when the two of you can meet, and be sure that you are totally alone. The place is important. It can be anywhere, but ideally it will be someplace that holds special significance for you and your husband.

Vow No. 1: Your Private Divorce

Husband: Stand facing your wife, take both of her hands, and repeat these vows out loud, looking directly into her eyes:

In many ways you have been a bitter disappointment to me. I have often failed you too. At times our marriage has seemed disastrous. I do not wish to bear this pain any longer. I hereby reject that part of you which has been a poor wife. To signify that the destructive part of our marriage is truly over, I return to you the ring you gave me on our wedding day. (Remove the wedding ring from your finger and place it in your wife's open palm.)

Wife: Remain facing your husband, take both of his hands, and repeat these vows out loud, looking directly into his eyes:

In many ways you have been a bitter disappointment to me. I have often failed you too. At times our marriage has seemed disastrous. I do not wish to bear this pain any longer. I hereby reject that part of you which has been a poor husband. To signify that the destructive part of our marriage is truly over, I return to you the ring you gave me on our wedding day. (Remove your wedding band/engagement ring from your finger and place it in your husband's open palm.)

Vow No. 2: Dying to Self

Husband, then wife: Speak aloud to God as your mate listens:

Dear God, I have sinned against my spouse. Even more, I have sinned against You. I believe You sent Your Son, Jesus Christ, to die on a cross and pay for my sins. Because He is God, I believe He rose from the dead on the third day and lives today.

Jesus, I now accept what You did for me on the Cross. I ask You to take away all my sins, including those I have committed against my spouse. Please come to live inside me. Give me the power to overcome my weaknesses and to become a totally new person. I hereby resign all control over my life. From this moment forward I will follow You until You take me to heaven when I die. Amen.

Vow No. 3: Remarriage

Husband: Stand facing your wife, take both of her hands, and repeat these vows out loud, looking directly into her eyes:

Beginning with this moment, I wipe the slate clean. I grant you a fresh start. I will never bring up the past to you again. With God's help, I will eradicate the past from my mind.

With this ring I make you my wife. (Slip the ring on her finger.) *I will do everything in my power to make you happy. I belong to you alone until we are separated by death. Before God, our witness, this is my solemn vow to you.*

Wife: Stand facing your husband, take both of his hands, and repeat these vows out loud, looking directly into his eyes:

Beginning with this moment, I wipe the slate clean. I grant you a fresh start. I will never bring up the past to you again. With God's help, I will eradicate the past from my mind.

With this ring I make you my husband. (Slip the ring on his finger.) *I will do everything in my power to make you happy. I belong to you alone until we are separated by death. Before God, our witness, this is my solemn vow to you.*

It is my prayer that you will commit to saving your marriage and that you have learned ways to strengthen your relationship with your husband and with God. God bless you.

Questions for Reflection

1. What unresolved conflict, long-

standing issues, or excess baggage are you aware of in your marriage?

2. While others may look at your circumstances and decide you're justified in seeking a legal divorce, can you see that what you may need is to put your present marriage behind you and start fresh?

3. Can you even imagine a marriage where the hurts, conflict, and strife is forgiven and forgotten, and you *can* resolve, renew, and recommit your marriage to God?

4. The vows in this chapter are powerful and binding. They may seem overwhelming and extreme. But ask yourself: do I want to continue the way things are, or do I want a radical change that will bring healing and wholeness to my marriage?

Scripture Meditations

"So don't lose a minute in building on what you've been given, complementing your basic faith with good character, spiritual understanding, alert discipline, passionate patience, reverent wonder, warm friendliness, and generous love, each dimension fitting into and developing the others. With these qualities active and growing in your lives, no grass will grow under your feet, no day will pass without its rewards as you mature in your experience of our Master Jesus. Without these qualities you can't see what's right before you, oblivious that your old sinful life has been wiped off the books. So, friends, confirm God's invitation to you, his choice to you. Don't put it off; do it now. Do this, and you'll have your life on a firm footing, the streets paved and the way wide open into the eternal kingdom of our Master and Savior, Jesus Christ" (2 Pet. 1:5-11).

My Journal

_____

_____

_____

_____

_____

_____

_____

_____

_____

_____

_____

_____

_____

_____

_____

_____

_____

_____

_____

_____

_____

_____

_____

_____

_____

_____

_____

_____

_____

_____

_____

_____

_____

_____

_____

_____

ENDNOTES

How Did I Get Here?

1. Randy Carlson, *Starved for Affection* (Wheaton, Ill.: Tyndale House Publishers, 2005), 75-76.

Accountability

1. James Dobson, *The Complete Marriage and Family Home Reference Guide* (Wheaton, Ill.: Tyndale House Publishers, 2000), 363.

2. Judith S. Wallerstein and Joan B. Kelly, *Surviving the Breakup* (New York: Basic Books, 1980), 33.

3. Ibid., 48.

4. Ibid., 236.

5. Ibid., 46.

6. Ibid., 211.

7. Nancy Cobb and Connie Grigsby, *The Best Thing I Ever Did for My Marriage* (Sisters, Oreg.: Multnomah Publishers, 2003), 146.

Expectations, Discontent, and Unconditional Love

1. James Dobson, *Straight Talk* (Sisters, Oreg.: Multnomah Publishers, 1995).

2. Nancy Groom, *From Bondage to Bonding* (Colorado Springs, Colo.: NavPress Publishers, 1991), 16.

3. Marsha Means, *Living with Your Husband's Secret Wars* (Grand Rapids: Revell, 1999), 51.

4. "God's Design for Marriage," Focus on the Family Website http:www.family.org/married/growth/aD028530.cfm. Used by permission.

5. Ibid.

6. Nancy Leigh DeMoss, excerpted from "Dealing with Unfulfilled Longings" (FamilyLife website: www.familylife.com/articles/article_detail.asp?id=98).

7. Carlson, *Starved for Affection,* 75-76.

Three Keys to Surrender

1. Theda Hlavka, *Saying I Do Was the Easy Part: Secrets to a Dynamic and Fulfilling Marriage* (Nashville: Broadman and Holman Publishers, 2001), 50-52. Used by permission.

2. Adapted from the FamilyLife Weekend to Remember workbook, 67.

3. "How Can I Resolve Conflict Well in My Marriage?" by Dennis and Barbara Rainey, FamilyLife.com. Used by permission.

4. Ney Bailey, "Cursing and Blessing" (Real FamilyLife Transcript, December 1997).

5. Martha Peace, *The Excellent Wife* (Bemidji, Minn.: Focus Publishing, 1995, 1999), 94-96.

6. Nancy Leigh DeMoss, *Lies Women Believe* (Chicago: Moody Publishers, 2001). Used by permission.

A New Twist on Submission

1. Hlavka, *Saying I Do,* 37.

2. "Understanding Your Husband" by Barbara Rainey, FamilyLife.com. Used by permission. www.familylife.com/articles/article_detail.asp?id=174.

3. Quoted in Nancy Cobb and Connie Grigsby, *The Best Thing I Ever Did for My Marriage,* author unknown (Sisters, Oreg.: Multnomah Publishers, 2003), 255-56.

Learning to Be Content

1. James Dobson, *Straight Talk to Men* (Sisters, Oreg.: Multnomah Publishers, 1984, 1991), 146.

2. Peace, *Excellent Wife,* 60-61.

3. Means, *Living with Your Husband's Secret Wars,* 58.

4. "Becoming a Family of Purpose," by Dennis and Barbara Rainey, FamilyLife.com. Used by permission.

Praying Scripture

1. Stormie Omartian, *The Power of a Praying Wife* (Eugene, Oreg.: Harvest House Publishers, 1997).

Your Legacy

1. "A Family Restoration Must Begin with Individual Sacrifice" by Dennis Rainey. Used by permission.

2. Tim Stafford, "Never Mind the Joneses" (Downers Grove, Ill.: InterVarsity Pres, 2004). Used by permission.

Starting Over

1. Steven Schwambach, *Tough Talk to a Stubborn Spouse* (Lincoln, Nebr.: iUniverse, 2001), 279-85.

My Journal

_____

_____

_____

_____

_____

_____

_____

_____

_____

_____

_____

_____

_____

_____

_____

_____

_____

_____

_____

_____

_____

_____

_____

_____

_____

_____

_____

_____

_____

_____

_____

_____

_____

_____

_____

_____

_____

_____

_____

_____

_____

_____

_____

_____

_____

_____

_____

_____

_____

_____

_____

_____

_____

_____

_____

_____

_____

_____

_____

_____

_____

_____

A 2003 ECPA Gold Medallion Finalist

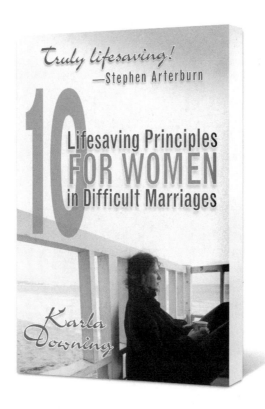

Regardless of the specific problems in your marriage, this book will help you find peace and confidence.

Karla Downing gives you the principles needed to overcome your sense of powerlessness and ultimately improve your life.

10 Lifesaving Principles for Women in Difficult Marriages
By Karla Downing
ISBN-13: 978-0-8341-2050-1

BEACON HILL PRESS
OF KANSAS CITY

Available wherever books are sold.

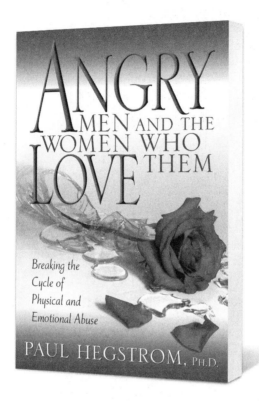

There is Hope.

In *My Husband Has a Secret*, Molly Ann Miller shares her personal struggle with her husband's sexual betrayal and offers compassion, comfort,
and encouragement for women in similar situations. She doesn't offer
easy answers. She doesn't even claim to be past the struggle herself. But
she does point the way to a loving Savior who offers hope and healing
to everyone involved and who will lead you on the difficult journey to
wholeness and peace.

My Husband Has a Secret
Finding Healing for the Betrayal of Sexual Addiction
By Molly Ann Miller
ISBN-13: 978-0-8341-2184-3

BEACON HILL PRESS
OF KANSAS CITY